HIMALAYA
The Secret of the Golden Tara

The teaching of the Buddha is
that you are your own master,
that all depends on yourself.

THE 14TH DALAI LAMA

CONTENTS

THE DALAI LAMA

MESSAGE OF HIS HOLINESS THE 14TH DALAI LAMA

The region of the Himalaya is home to a unique culture and life style. This is due to a number of different factors, the most important of which is the natural environment. On the one hand, the rough climate with its extremes and the difficult landscapes is responsible for the inhabitants being tough, flexible and inventive people. On the other hand, because of the immensity of the country and the relatively low population density, the peoples of the Himalaya region are not affected by the burdens and tensions that are troubling our neighbors living in cramped surroundings.

On top of that, due to the lack of Tarmac roads and automobile transport – until recently – life has been passing at a slow pace. To a wide extent, there is no tendency toward hurry, which is such an obvious feature of our modern cities. The seasons play a decisive role in the rhythm of life.

Although well acquainted with the Tibetans, their customs and their lifestyles, I observed that the majority of the peoples of the Himalayan region are – regardless of the conditions – similarly well behaved, modest, content and steadfast in times of hardship. One reason for these favorable characteristics is – as I have already mentioned – the outer environment and secondly the Buddhist faith. I am deeply convinced that the teachings of love, goodness and tolerance, the rule of non-violence, and especially the Buddhist view that everything is interdependent serve to enhance inner peace.

I am very pleased to see that Dieter Glogowski has captured, in his excellent photographs, a lot of this patient and unhurried life style, which is such an important part of the Himalayan peoples' character. His pictures have a strong message: they are a vision alive that make those who look at them familiar with and appreciate a far away part of the world, of which many probably have heard but few will actually visit.

THE 14TH DALAI LAMA
July 30, 2004

Buddhism in the Himalaya

By Katharina Sommer

Where the barren high plains of the Himalaya lie, the dimensions of which are hardly comprehensible, the clouds move over the deepest gorges and the highest mountains of the world. Where the holy places are uncountable, where the wind plays with thousands of prayer flags, where day in and day out hundreds of prayer wheels spin, there, sits the home of Tibetan Buddhism. Where else is spirituality so distinct and existence animated in this way? Where else is religion indivisible from people's everyday life? Well over 20 million Buddhists in the Himalayan region practice a path enabling every individual – through compassion and vigilance – to overcome the veils of delusion and be relieved from the cycle of existences: because Buddha represents enlightenment.

BUDDHA SHAKYAMUNI'S LIFE STORY

The traditional life story of the historical Buddha Shakyamuni, who is dated from 450 to 370 BC, is influenced by diverse intentions and by the fact that historiography was not beginning until late after his activities. It shows a picture, partly historical, partly rooted in myths.

It is said, that the whole world held its breath when Siddhartha Gautama was, accompanied by cosmic signs, supernaturally born from his mother Mayadevi in Lumbini, which is situated in the south of what is Nepal today. Some Brahmins recognized that the child had the birthmarks of a 'special being' and they prophesized he would be the King of Kings or a great spiritual master. However, Siddhartha's father Suddhodana, the Raja of the Shakya republic of Kapilavastu, was planning to educate his son to be a worldly ruler. Therefore, he tried to connect him to family and home with all the conveniences and trappings a wealthy man could provide. Nevertheless, as the years passed, Siddhartha's curiosity toward the world outside the palace walls was growing and he undertook four excursions in a splendid carriage.

On those occasions, for the first time he saw people with the signs of old age and sickness, and he witnessed a dead man and an ascetic. He was transformed through these encounters because he realized that authentic living is connected to suffering, and he decided to exchange his sheltered life of luxury with the quest for realization. For no one was able to answer his questions about the meaning of human existence.

One night around midnight, he secretly escaped from the palace. In the robes of a wandering monk, he joined five ascetics and went to see two great masters. Although these masters taught him the practices of meditation, they did not discuss the causes of suffering. In the following six years, Siddhartha underwent strict fasting, feeding on no more than a corn of rice and a drop of water. Completely drained, "abdominal wall and spine nearly touching," he concluded that, with a mind weakened by ascetic practices, he would never achieve clarity, and that extremes never lead to a solution. As Siddhartha started to eat again, his five companions turned their backs on him because for them his action meant defeat. Then he settled beneath a fig tree in a place called Bodh-Gaya. Even if "his flesh and blood would get dry" he was determined not to rise from his seat before he had attained complete enlightenment.

During the following three nights he overcame the temptations of Mara, the Lord of desires, and thus liberated, he had achieved at the same time the knowledge of liberation. He had become a Buddha. "Nothing exists from its own part," this absolute truth was revealed to him. He had realized the cycle of becoming and ceasing, which is the cause of suffering and keeps people in ignorance of the nature of reality, and he had realized that every human being has the potential for realization and thus can overcome his existence in suffering. This is what he expressed in the Four Noble Truths, which were to become the guidelines of all Buddhist followers. These are:

THE TRUTH OF SUFFERING: BIRTH, SICKNESS, SEPARATION, DEATH, OR WISHES UNFULFILLED, ALL THIS IS SUFFERING.

The Truth of the Origin of Suffering: craving for power, wealth, passion, pleasures and other emotions lead from one rebirth to the next.

The Truth of the Cessation of Suffering: when renouncing from craving one can overcome suffering.

The Truth of the Path leading to the Transcendence of Suffering: in order to suspend the compulsion of being reborn again and again, the Buddha taught the Eightfold Noble Path, which requires a focus on the right outlook, right intention, right speech, right action, right livelihood,

right pursuit, right mindfulness and right concentration. Buddha Shakyamuni was hesitant to share his realization with others, but the God Brahma persuaded him to "turn the wheel of the Dharma," and thus he held his first sermon in the deer park of Sarnath. He had never proclaimed any dogma, because according to his teaching delusion may only be overcome through the reflections of one's own mind: "Who merely takes on what is known already, joins the group of the blind."

For the following 50 years wandering about in North India with many disciples – even his five former companions came to join him –, he spread the Dharma and shared his realization with the people. Place number four which has become a religious site for the sake of the Buddha is Kusinara, the place where he passed away. Beginning with the enlightenment of the historical Buddha Shakyamuni, the history of Buddhism was set into motion, which made generations of people follow the path of spiritual development with the help of his teachings.

THE SPREAD OF BUDDHISM

There are several reasons why the teachings of the Buddha were spreading from North India to large regions of the whole country within a short period. In India, there was a period of social change: nomads were settling down, cities were developing. Such new structures of life were intensifying social differences – a perfect breeding ground for the Buddhist philosophy. For regardless of the hierarchies of the caste system, the new teachings were open to everybody, whether lay person or monk of a monastic community. The policy of King Ashoka, whose leadership was reaching as far as South India in the third century BC, was decisive in this respect. As a Buddhist follower, he was granting religious tolerance to his subjects. He did not install Buddhism as a state religion but Buddhist ethics were the basis of his leadership. He wanted to bring the new teachings 'to every corner of the world,' thus he sent out messengers in all directions. His son Mahinda introduced Buddhism to Sri Lanka. From there monks and traders took the new religion via Myanmar, Thailand, Cambodia, Laos and Vietnam along the Silk Road to China, Korea, Japan and Mongolia. In the course of the 7th century, missionaries eventually reached the Himalayan region as well.

Not only because of its "1,000 faces," nearly 360 million followers worldwide practice Buddhism in its different varieties today. Already in Ashoka's times diverse interpretations of the essential nature of things and different opinions in questions of discipline had lead to schisms and new views about the path to realization. The large area of influence, that is to say, the confrontation with pre-Buddhist ethnic religions and their integration into the new teachings, made two main divisions survive: the Hinayana and the Mahayana, which had arisen somewhat later.

Among the different schools of the Hinayana, the Theravada tradition alone has prevailed mainly in South Asia and South-East Asia until today. As opposed to the Mahayana, the Hinayana refers to the basic philosophical idea that our existence and the suffering connected to it are real. By one's own strength exclusively, by renouncing from the world and leading a monastic life, it is possible for an individual human being to get free from the cycle of rebirths and reach Nirvana. This idea corresponds with the Arhat ideal of the Hinayana. The Buddha, who has manifested in this world, is considered a human being and a teacher.

On the contrary, in the Mahayana the world is viewed as a projection of the mind and has no substance. Monks and lay people alike can experience enlightenment, and on top of that: the Bodhisattva ideal of the Mahayana stresses the compassion of precisely those who have reached enlightenment, because voluntarily they remain within the cycle of rebirths in order to lead all beings toward liberation. The Buddha is considered in a different way, as well. There is not only one Buddha, but there are countless, and it is possible to attain their transcendent spirituality through prayer.

From another division, the Vajrayana, sometimes explained as a third main section, sometimes explained as a tantric branch of the Mahayana, Tibetan Buddhism, also named Lamaism, has developed. Its spreading in the Himalayan region is mainly ascribed to the scholar, magician, and tantric Padmasambhava, who in Tibet is venerated as the "Precious Teacher".

Padmasambhava and the spreading of Buddhism in Tibet

Countless legends are connected to the life and activity of Padmasambhava. It is said that he was born in a miraculous way from a lotus flower in the middle of a lake in what is West Kashmir today. He was accepted by Indrabhuti, the ruler of the mythical kingdom of Uddiyana, as his own child, in the hope of making him his successor. However, Padmasambhava realized that he would not be of much benefit to the people as a monarch. Therefore, he intentionally behaved in such a way that he became a disgrace to his father's palace and had to be banished.

This was followed by many years of roaming about. He became deeply involved in the teachings of the Buddha and went into retreat at unusual places of meditation for spiritual practices. From Gurus and masters he received instructions and, eventually, the most important tantric teachings. Only few are initiated into such rituals and practices because a tantric master has the full responsibility for the spiritual development of his disciple. The main point of tantrism is the experience of the cosmic union of power and energy, of wisdom and method, of female and male. The union of energies transforming into mental power open up the doors for the experience of one's own Buddha nature, thus, leading to the path of enlightenment. Padmasambhava had become such an important tantric master that his reputation went as far as Tibet. Trisong Detsen, the King of Tibet, found himself confronted with problems in matters of domestic policy during his reign toward the end of the 8th century, which were rooted in tensions between aristocracy and king as well as between Buddhism and the ethnic belief of the animistic Bon religion. Attracted by the Buddhist teachings, Trisong Detsen was hoping for Padmasambhava's support, who was able, in the appearance of eight different manifestations, partly extremely wrathful, to defeat the demons and spirits of the Bon religion. Padmasambhava complied with the wishes of the king. He was ready to travel before the invitation had reached him, because he had foreseen it.

It is not for his triumph over the spiritual forces of the Bon alone that Padmasambhava is venerated as one of the most ambivalent figures of Buddhism, as an emanation of Buddha Shakyamuni, and as a second Buddha. On his initiative, the first Buddhist monastery of Tibet was built in Samye, and the scriptures of the Buddhist canon were translated into Tibetan. Based on the idea of a gradual path, which leads to the experience of the absolute nature by means of continual increase of discipline and spiritual exercise, Padmasambhava established Vajrayana Buddhism in Tibet, which is a synthesis of Bon elements and the teaching of the Buddha. He founded several monastic communities, where his teaching tradition was able to survive the persecution of Buddhist followers during the 9th century. For the Nyingma school, the first of Tibetan Buddhism – also called 'the Old School' – his teaching was to become fundamental.

The four schools of Tibetan Buddhism

The Nyingma school is one of the four philosophical traditions of Tibetan Buddhism, which developed from the 10th to the 12th century. The Nyingmapas are the least hierarchical among the four schools, and they rely on the tradition of Dzogchen, the Great Perfection, as their most important instruction. Based on the idea that the purity of the mind is present and simply has to be recognized, the Dzogchen teachings comprise meditation and yoga practices in order to realize the nature of mind. Besides the Buddhist canonical scriptures, they rely on texts which have been hidden by Padmasambhava himself. Such scriptures hidden all over Tibet to be discovered in later times are a special feature of the Nyingma school. The scholar Longchenpa compiled and commented on Dzogchen in the 14th century. His work has shaped the teaching tradition of the school until today. Among the rediscovered texts, "Padmasambhava's treasures," there is the "Bardo Thodol" – "The Tibetan Book of the Dead." Its instructions are read to the dying or whispered into their ears to help them realize the nature of their own mind.

As were the teachings of Padmasambhava integrated into the philosophy of the Nyingma school, the Kadampa instructions of Atisha, a scholar from Bengal who had come to Tibet in the beginning of the 11th century, were absorbed by the Sakya, Kagyu, and Gelug schools. The Kadampa tradition is mainly concerned with the proper interpretation of the Buddhist scriptures, with keeping the purity of the monastic order, as well as emphasizing the idea of compassion toward all beings.

The Sakya school, named after their main seat, Sakya Monastery, founded by Konchok Gyalpo, relies on the system of Lamdre. Here, teachings and practices are based on the Vajrayana principle that the path itself represents its goal at the same time. By means of constructing and sponsoring further monasteries, which granted protection and support to many scholars, busy writing and translating activities have developed since the 11th century. Until the Chinese occupation of Tibet in 1959, the Sakya monasteries were home to one of the most comprehensive collections of manuscripts of all Buddhist traditions. Monks could only take a small part of the library to North India on their escape and save it from being seized by Mao Zedong's Red Army.

The founding of the Kagyu school is traced back to the translator Marpa, who brought the fundamental propositions of this order from India to Tibet during the 11th century. Marpa's disciple Milarepa, whose life story is characterized by extremely hard trials and is remarkably comparable to that of the Buddha, is venerated in Tibet not only as a poet and mystic but also as a holy being. He was practicing the meditation techniques of the Great Seal as well as the Six Doctrines, which his disciple Gampopa later attached to the Kadampa tradition of Atisha as the future teaching tradition of the Kagyu order. After the founding of Tsurphu Monastery in 1183, within the Kagyu school the Karma Kagyu split off as a sub-school whose spiritual authority, the Karmapa, represents the oldest tradition of reincarnated lamas in Tibet. Since the 15th century, the Karmapas as well as the Dalai Lamas have been considered manifestations of Avalokiteshvara, the Bodhisattva of compassion.

Whereas for the Kagyupas meditation techniques are characteristic, logic and the intellectual discussion of the Buddhist teachings are prevalent for the Gelug school. Tsongkhapa, like Padmasambhava venerated as a manifestation of Manjushri, the Bodhisattva of wisdom, was one of the most important Buddhist scholars. In 1409 with the founding of the large Ganden Monastery, followed by Drepung and Sera Monasteries, he established the Gelug order. Following the tradition of the Kadampa, he reformed the monks' disciplinary rules by committing them to intensive study of the scriptures and to celibacy. His 25 volume "Lamrim," the gradual path to enlightenment, has been among the required reading of the Gelugpas until today.

THE DALAI LAMAS

By the end of the 16th century, Sonam Gyatso, an abbot of the Gelugpas' Drepung Monastery, was trying to win Altai Khan, the ruler of the Mongols, as a protective patron for Tibet due to domestic political conflicts. For this purpose, he declared the Khan a reincarnation of Khublai Khan and himself a former leader of the Sakya. Thus, confirmed in his claim to power he conferred the Mongolian honorary title Dalai Lama, Ocean of Wisdom, on Sonam in 1578. Following this, the Buddhist teaching became more and more influential in Mongolia.

The title Dalai Lama was also meant to commemorate the great period of Tsongkhapa. Therefore two former abbots of Drepung Monastery, Tsongkhapa's nephew Gendun Dub as well as Gendun Gyatso were conferred the titles of first and second Dalai Lama retrospectively. Thus, Sonam went down in history as the third Dalai Lama. As a reincarnation of the first two and as a manifestation of Avalokiteshvara at the same time, his honorary title Dalai Lama became the lineage title of continually reincarnating lamas.

The fifth Dalai Lama came to play a special role because, during the unstable times of domestic as well as foreign policy problems, as the Great Fifth he established with diplomacy and foresight the rule of the lamas and strengthened the Gelug leadership over the whole of Tibet. By bestowing an honorary title above his own on his teacher, he established the lineage of the Panchen lamas, who reincarnate as a manifestation of Amitabha, one of the most important Buddhas of the Mahayana. At first appointed the spiritual representative of the Dalai Lamas, the Panchen Lama has fulfilled politi-cal duties since the 20th century as well. Today's spiritual and political authority for Tibetans is His Holiness, the 14th Dalai Lama. Since 1959, he has lived in exile in Dharamsala, North India.

BY AIR MAIL
PARAVION

DIETER GLOGOWSKI
MITTELSTRASSE 1
61169 FRIEDBERG
GERMANY

When the iron bird flies and horses ride on wheels
a power from the North will appear,
destroy our religion,
and proclaim itself the ruler of the world.
This will be the time when the teaching of the Buddhas
will enter the hearts of the people in the West.

TIBETAN PROPHECY

A LETTER FROM SONAM

For Dieter
I am over 90 years of age now and I can feel
that my body is getting weaker.
The time for me to die is approaching.
There is an important secret I have to tell you
before I leave this world.
Therefore you have to come to Lingshed as quickly
as possible. That's the message I have for you.
I am hoping and praying that we will meet soon.
Tashi delek
Sonam Yospel
Year 2002, 9th month, 5th day

December 16, 2002:

There is an airmail letter in my mailbox. The stamps are Indian; next to them, I recognize the handwriting of my old friend Sonam Yospel, who is a 95-year-old monk of Lingshed Monastery in Ladakh. My eyes follow along the lines of his message. He wants me to come and see him – it's about an important secret – he wants my help. Deep in thought I turn the envelope around and I read: "Om Ah Hung Benza Guru Pema Siddhi Hung," Padmasambhava's protection mantra. This I will need. I look out of the window, thick snow flakes are playing in the wind. "…Come quickly…," his words are clear, the mantra was carefully chosen.

We were reciting Padmasambhava's mantra together many times. My thoughts flow back to Lingshed. Jackdaws were circling above Sonam's hermitage, summer flowers were emitting a sweet scent and the conch shell was calling the monks to hold puja. I could hear some novice monks laughing. A five

it on your body, it will protect you! Maybe you will need it one day." Sonam pressed his forehead against mine. This was two years ago. I pick up the phone and book a flight to Delhi. Departure February 8, 2003: I will spend only half a night at the airport in Delhi and take a direct flight to Leh, Ladakh's

days walk away from the nearest road, the yellow-hat monastery of Lingshed lies hidden at an altitude of 4,000 meters (13,120 feet) in the Northern part of the Indian Himalaya. I have known Sonam for more than 15 years now. He had spent most of his life as a monk in Lingshed. Only once, that's what he was telling me, he had gone to Tibet for 15 years – following the old tradition to study Tibetan philosophy.

capital, immediately the following morning. For the flight-captain this means observing the visual flight rules all along the 1,000 kilometers (620 miles) across the whole Himalayan mountain range from south to north. During the winter months, air traffic is the only means of connection with the outer world for the inhabitants of Leh. Up until May the high passes are covered with snow and impassible.

Sweet are the fruits of hope that is fulfilled.
But who can let go even of hope, lives in peace.

Saying these words, he put an old Tibetan amulet in my hands. "I had it made when I was staying in Tibet for my studies. Wear

For the fourth time, I will go on foot to Lingshed during winter, over the frozen river Chaddar.

The sleds crunch loudly on the mirror-like smooth and icy surface of the Chaddar. A cold wind blows in our faces. Step by
step we try to find our path on the bizarrely formed ice cover
of the Chaddar, the river in the shadow, as it is called by the
people of Ladakh and Zanskar during winter time. For a distance of 180 kilometers (112 miles) at an altitude of 3,500
meters (11,480 feet), it meanders through a steep gorge. During the seven-months-long bitter cold winter, the river is the
only connection between the former kingdom of Ladakh and
Zanskar. Temperatures often drop below minus 37 degrees Celsius. Five cold and frosty days of arduous walking are ahead of
us, with the prospect of storms, fresh snow and the danger of
avalanches. Tsewang, the monk, together with three farmers
Tundup, Karma and Tashi are my companions. They have done
this stretch of the Chaddar countless times before. "Every time
the same, but different!" Tashi says jokingly. With a long stick,
he hits the ice cover and checks its thickness by means of
sound. For hours in the same rhythm, we walk the path winding through the gorge. Then the first problem occurs ahead of
us! The river is "open"! "Chu tangmo – cold water!" Tsewang
slaps my shoulder with a laugh. Nodding with a sigh, I start
taking off my shoes and pants. Half naked we cross the icy cold
water.

You can find a new path only if you have the courage to lose sight of the riverbanks.

This is what I write in my daybook that night. Silently the
campfire crackles, our shadows dance on the cave walls. "Life is
suffering!" Karma jokes and continues reading his sutras. I
plunge into a well-deserved sleep.

"Dieter-la, julley, tscha tsatpa?" I peep out of my sleeping bag. Far down below us the Chaddar rushes by. Yesterday, not before late in the evening, we reached Bagula-Bou cave to find shelter. It is situated 70 meters (230 feet) above the river and has space for at least 20 persons. When we arrived, a fire was already burning. Rigzin Dorje and his brother Lobsang welcomed us with a hot Tukpa, Ladakh's traditional noodle soup. The two Zanskaris live in the small village of Pidmu; since four days they had been on their way to Leh. We were exchanging news, drinking butter tea, talking and laughing until late that night.

care – many people in the Western world would consider life under such circumstances to be potentially dangerous. Surprisingly, the idea of peace and tranquility alone without any distractions and busyness is a cause of unrest and anxiousness for them. "Nobody at home," Sogyal Rinpoche would say, "always out." We do not know ourselves because rarely we are within ourselves.

"Tscha tsatpa?" I rub the sleep from my eyes; Tsewang offers me a cup of hot tea. "Kyaks tangpo gyala – the ice is strong!" he shouts and carries the loaded sledge down the slope, followed by the others.

We can experience the course of our lives as heaven or as hell – all depends on our perception.

These words of Pema Chödrön, who is a nun, go through my mind. The hard winter in Ladakh with all its forces of nature, the remoteness of the villages, living in a region without electricity, without modern communication facilities and medical

I pack my backpack, fill my bottle with tea, and extinguish the fire. From the cave entrance I take a photograph of my companion's line of helpers taking their initial steps. In spite of the first sunrays, the air is cold and the snow is hard like concrete.

On the fifth day, we leave the cracking ice cover of the Chaddar and turn into the steep Lingshed side valley. After a climb of four hours, we reach the village. About 50 monks and 30 novices belonging to the yellow-hat tradition, the virtuous, live here in Lingshed Monastery, which is 500 years old. From far away already, we can hear the penetrating sound of the conch shell. The gompa courtyard is filled with the bustle of activity. Unmistakably, I see young monks cram up sutra texts, which they learn by heart. The old doors of the hermitages creak, monks and novices leaving their small huts make their way up to the prayer hall for puja. Warming rays of sunshine float into the room helping one forget about the coldness of these icy winter days. Ganda and Dorje ? bell and scepter ?, the most important ritual implements, are kept at ready. They stand for the union of polar opposites: for the female and the male principles, for wisdom and method.

"Where is Sonam Yospel?" I ask Lama Sandup. "He is sick; he is waiting for you at his place. Let's go see him," he replies. Sandup sounds serious. "Sonam-la, tashi delek!" we greet him in one voice. The heavy door opens. Motup, a small novice, shows me through the dark hallway to the stone steps. My hands reach for the familiar wooden handrail. I climb up the steep irregular steps, past the tiny winter kitchen, from where it smells of butter tea.

I hear Sonam's voice murmuring, whilst climbing further up to the roof terrace. There he sits, the ivory-color rosary in his hands, reciting mantras.

I address him with, "Julley, nga toks rgatpo – I greet you, my old friend."

"Julley, nga toks zhonu – I greet you, my young friend!" he replies with a laugh.

I offer him a Tibetan white scarf. Sonam reaches for my shoulders and presses his forehead against mine.

tortured to death. Thousands of monks escaped from Ganden. The first wave of destruction came in 1961. Systematically, Buddha statues were smashed and precious metals like copper, brass, silver and gold were brought to China. In addition, many monks were ordered to put down their robes and marry. Most chose to go into exile and decided to escape. Thousands of Tibetans died crossing over the Himalayan high passes on their way to Sikkim, Bhutan, or Nepal.

In 1966, China proclaimed the Cultural Revolution. The night

Life is fleeting like a dewdrop on a blade of grass.

"Good that you are here," he begins to talk: "More than 50 years ago, I went to study Buddhist philosophy at Ganden Monastery in Tibet. Many monks came there to be educated in Buddhist dialectics. I reached Ganden in 1950, one day ahead of China's invasion into Tibet. At first, this did not affect us much there in Central Tibet because in the beginning the Chinese occupied Tibet's Eastern parts. However, in the winter of 1951, the first Chinese military convoy reached Lhasa. They called it 'return of the Tibetan people to the family of the Motherland' or 'liberation of the Tibetan people!' False slogans of China's propaganda. Again and again Chinese patrols forced their way into the monastery saying that we would exploit the people and that no Tibetan would be allowed to work on our fields anymore. If we wanted to eat, we would have to take care of food ourselves.

Horrible news was coming from East Tibet, about mass executions of monks and nuns, looting and the destruction of monasteries. Initially, the reason why China avoided unrest in the large monasteries around Lhasa was probably tactical. After all, at that time Ganden had more than 8,000 monks. Eventually though, on March 18, 1959, the people of Lhasa revolted. Two days later, the Chinese military hit back without mercy. Within the first three days of the action, more than 10,000 Tibetans came to die, by October 1959, the death toll reached already 90,000. Detentions, torture and public humiliation were the order of the day. 'Fighting sessions' were held during which we were urged to condemn other monks. If you refused, they would hang you on a tree by your hands tied together on your back. Tibetans were beaten and kicked, often

that the Red Guards first attacked the monastery with grenades, I decided to escape to Ladakh. On our farewell the abbot Norsang Gyeche gave a small golden Tara statue to me. He said, 'Sonam, you are from Ladakh. On your way home you will probably pass the Holy Mountain Kailash. Take this Tara to the Inner Mandala of Kailash for the protection of Tibet, please hurry up!'

It was a very beautiful Green Tara. My student Pasang accompanied me, he was from Nepal and wanted to return together with me. One week later, we came to Shigatse. I tried to buy provisions at the market, while Pasang was waiting for me in a hiding place and guarding the Tara. I was still wearing my red monk's robes. This was a disastrous mistake because I ran straight into the arms of a Chinese patrol and was arrested. I have never seen Pasang Lama again. Like many other monks and nuns I was taken to a camp near Lhasa for 're-education.' During the nights we were secretly murmuring a prayer of the Indian master Shantideva:

'May those who go in dread have no more fear. May captives be unchained and now set free. And may the weak receive their strength. May living beings help each other in kindness.' Two years later, I was able to escape, meanwhile the Kailash became a restricted area. I went back to Lingshed.

You are very familiar with the Kailash region. Look for the Tara, find out if she has ever reached there, or look for Pasang Lama, he was from Melamchighyang Monastery. You can recognize him by his amulet because he is wearing the same as you." Sonam Yospel's hand softly touched the silver amulet on my chest. "Be cautious and take good care of yourself!"

Tara – Symbol and Teaching
By Katharina Sommer

Om Tare Tuttare Ture Svaha. Louder and louder the murmuring of the mantra fills the hallways of the Jokhang, Tibet's most holy temple complex in the heart of Lhasa. Om Tare Tuttare Ture Svaha. Louder and louder, the murmuring of the mantra reaches the ears of the little Tibetan boy Tashi Nyima, who shyly takes the hand of his grandmother Tsering Dolma. "Today we are going on a very special journey," she whispers full of awe. Her eyes are smiling.

So many generations of deeply religious Tibetans have passed through the same hallways and chapels before these two, for the Jokhang has been the most important destination of every pilgrimage since it was constructed in the 7th century during the rule of Songtsen Gampo. With good reason: on the one hand it contains numerous statues and paintings – each of its own inestimable value; on the other hand myths are woven around the origin of this spiritual place which are deeply connected to Songtsen Gampo and two of his queens: Bhrikuti from Nepal and Wen Cheng from China. Both being Buddhists, they had a decisive influence on the spreading and official establishment of their belief in Tibet, to the effect that all three of them were reborn in the Buddhist God realms after they had passed away. Since then and to this day, Songtsen Gampo, the first religious king of the country, is considered to be an incarnation of Avalokiteshvara, the Bodhisattva of compassion, whereas Bhrikuti is venerated as an emanation of the Green Tara and Wen Cheng as the White Tara. Among the 22 different manifestations of Tara, who were born, as the legend goes, from the tears which Avalokiteshvara had shed over the suffering in the world, the Green Tara and the White Tara have a very special meaning for Buddhists because of their symbolism and the teaching connected to it.

A thousand butter lamps are burning, their smell filling the room, as Tsering Dolma with her grandchild steps in front of the Tara statues. Strength and comfort can be felt, for the Green Tara is considered not only to be an embodiment of the historical Buddha Shakyamuni's mother, but a protection patroness of Tibet and at the same time a savioress from all suffering. She can give protection from actual threats as well as from the eight great terrors

of life, which obstruct the path to inner freedom and perfection:

– the lion of pride
– the elephant of delusion
– the fire of anger
– the snake of jealousy
– the robber of wrong view
– the shackles of miserliness
– the flood of desire
– the demon of doubt

The spiritual presence and compassionate energy of Tara is mirrored in the symbolic gestures of the figure. Such as the left leg of the Green Tara showing the meditation posture and the right stretching slightly to the front – ready to go, ready to act with compassion. Her left hand symbolizes fearlessness and the threefold refuge to Buddha, Dharma and Sangha; the right shows the gesture of granting goodwill. She holds blue lotus flowers in both hands and, as an expression of strength, life and purity, her whole body is surrounded by a sea of flowers.

The White Tara sitting in the traditional meditation posture symbolizes peace and wealth. As the "Seven-eyed Goddess," she has additional eyes on her forehead, on the palms of her hands and on her feet, by means of which she can see all the suffering of the world. The gesture of her left hand, which holds a lotus flower, expresses the granting of refuge, the right expresses generosity.

Deep in contemplation the Tibetan lady requests healing care and compassion. Tashi cannot understand his grandmother's words, but intuitively he grasps the meaning of this special journey: for the murmuring of the mantra is still filling the hallways of the Jokhang. In times before, it was only possible to recite it in one's mind, but a lot has changed in Tibet, and today the invocation of Tara with the request for protection has to be audible and powerful. Om Tare Tuttare Ture Svaha.

Left: A masterly thangka from the Norbulinka painting school near Dharamsala.
Right: Thangka of a Green Tara; Tara statue at Sera Monastery, South India; carved Green Tara in Bhutan; coloring of a Tara statue in Dharamsala.

TIBET IN EXILE

March 10, 2003, Bangalore, South India

"Believe me; what you see here is India's economically most prosperous city, the pride of our nation! This is where the heart of the Indian computer industry beats, we write the programs for half of the world." Ramesh Sigh shifts a good part of his body weight to my seat and presses his sweating face to the aircraft window: "Incredible, this city – jungle and skyscrapers – agriculture and microchips. India's Silicon Valley – here you can make money!" My Indian businessperson sinks back into his seat, his tired eyes surrounded by dark brown shadows. On his fingers, excessively magnificent rings sparkle and his paunch is witness to many a glass he drank. I close my eyes and Sogyal Rinpoche's provocative words come to my mind:

"Busyness is the laziness of the West!" With the businessman on my left and the Indian metropolis coming into view, the implications of this concept are not easy to grasp!
Bangalore Airport: noise, hectic rush, hands tugging at my luggage, tropical heat, 37 degrees Celsius. Tibet in exile? A gigantic monk appears: "Are you Mr. Daiter? My name is Tashi Sanshup, I'm your driver from Sera Monastery." It takes twelve hours to reach the exile monasteries of Ganden and Drepung near Mungod. More than 4,000 Tibetan monks live there, surrounded by villages and dense jungle, by water buffalos and tigers, banana fields and windmills. I am on my search for eye witnesses of Ganden Monastery's destruction.

After the people's revolt in Tibet and the escape of the Dalai Lama in 1959, tens of thousands of Tibetans had followed their spiritual leader into exile to India. Refugee camps were set up in the North Indian Himalaya region, in Nepal and in Sikkim. Even Switzerland accepted 3,000 Tibetans. When the Indian camps were too overcrowded to take in any further of the refugees who kept streaming in the Prime Minister at the time, Nehru, decided to offer them, there and then, the jungle areas near Bangalore. The first Tibetan colonies in South India were established in the beginning of the sixties.

"When we arrived, there was nothing but dense jungle – the water was nearly undrinkable, the hot and humid climate hardly bearable, and there were many wild elephants and tigers!" Softly Dolma Tsering lets her white rosary slide through her fingers: "Every day the men went to the jungle, felled trees, cleared the land. My husband and two of my children died from malaria one year after we had arrived. We were just not accustomed to such a tropical climate." Dolma Tsering is 71 years old. Her face expresses warmth and kindness: "In Tibet we had lived in a small village near Ganden. The air was fresh and cold, the view clear and limitless. My father had a flock of yaks and 200 goats. Every year at Losar time, the Tibetan New Year, we went to visit Ganden Monastery. My uncle was a monk there and a respected master of debate as well. Everybody liked him and appreciated his knowledge. Two weeks after the people's revolt had been suppressed, hundreds of Chinese soldiers flooded the monastery. They took brutal action against the monks, herded them together in dozens and deported them. Among them was my uncle, too. They insulted him, swore at him and accused him of being a counter revolutionist, one of the incorrigible kinds! We have never seen him since."

"Amala, Amala!" A little girl comes running. "We have lived here at the camp for three generation already. Now I only take care of my family and my three cows." She takes her grandchild on her arm with a laugh. I think of the Dalai Lama's words:

When people laugh, they are able to think.

The day is coming to an end. Young monks recite Buddhist scriptures in the fields. It is hard to get accustomed to red Tibetan monks' robes with banana trees in the background.

My research in Ganden and Drepung is without success. I happened to see the gigantic "neo-Tibetan rebuilt exile monasteries" with their concrete charm, but eye-witnesses to the destruction of Ganden Monastery are rare in this place. Tashi persuades me to take the nine-hour ride and continue to Bylakuppe, where Sera Monastery is situated, beside Ganden and Drepung the third important Gelug Monastery in South India.

"Welcome to Tibetian Refugee Settlement" it says on a torn banner at the corner of the road. We pass Village No. 1, which was founded in 1961. As the jungle was driven back, further villages had developed, each of them inhabited by some 300 Tibetan families. Today there are 17, Bylakuppe being one of the largest Tibetan settlements in India. More than 5,000 monks study there these days. The compound of the monastery has become so gigantic, meanwhile, that such a "building boom" could be critically put into question. Anyway, in an Internet café there is a notice posted on the wall with a quotation of His Holiness:

We do not need temples,
we do not need complicated philosophies.
Our hearts are our temples,
our philosophy is kindness.

The large exile monasteries are like monstrous representation objects to me. "Red people bring green money!" the rickshaw driver shouts at me whilst taking me to the Golden Temple in the early morning. It is the 15th day after Losar and today the largest thangka worldwide is to be unrolled. The streets are overcrowded with monks and nuns. Tibetans from all camps have arrived – as well as Indian beggars. At the entrance of Namdroling Monastery dozens of motorbikes are parked, their owners wearing red robes. How fitting Drukpa Rinpoche's words are: "Stop accumulating things if you want your life to be a success. The accumulation of material goods is nothing but a caricature of happiness. It is a distraction and a burden for the mind. Become light once more!"
I take the return flight to Delhi and go to Dharamsala following the invitation of the Dalai Lama.

TIBET IN EXILE   49

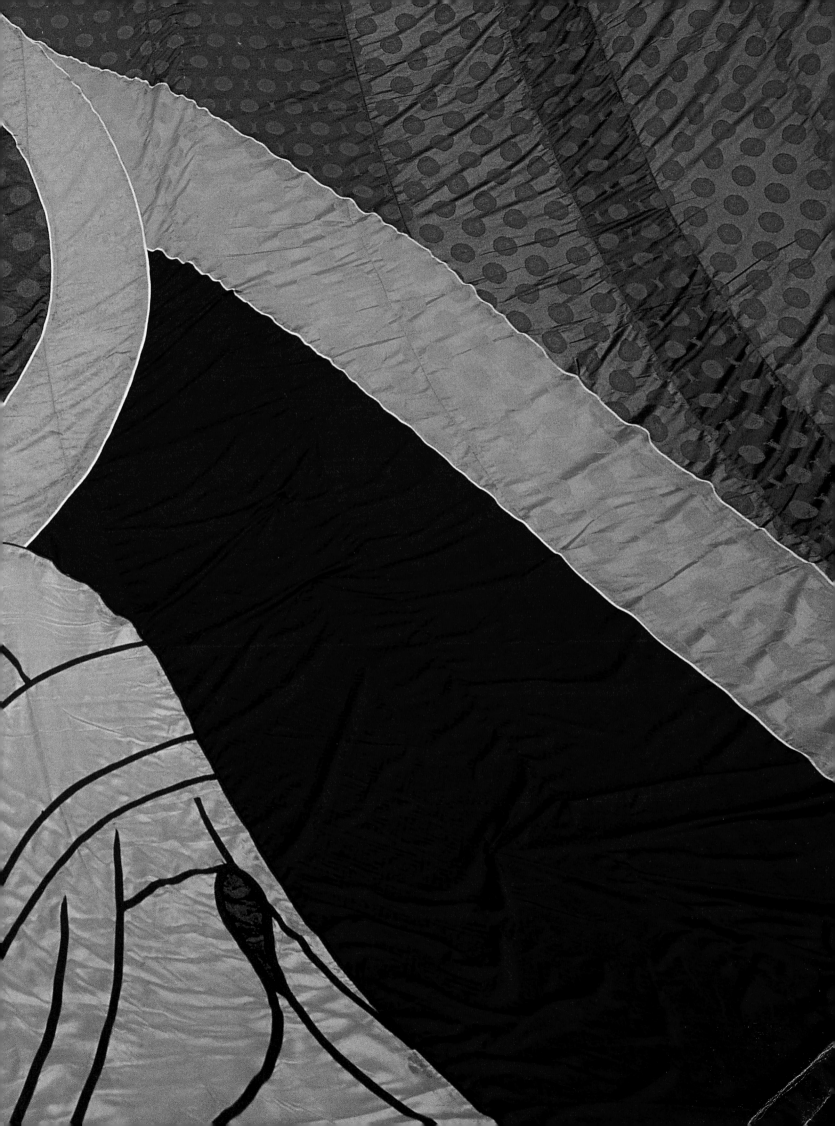

Debates
By Katharina Sommer

Even the youngest novices know that debating is great fun and a joyful activity, that juggling with propositions and refutations can mean laughter and joking. Especially for the Gelug school, logic, the teaching of consequent thinking and dialectics, among many other subjects, is part of every monastery's curriculum – because clear and independent ability to think is fundamental for understanding the teachings of the Buddha. Every afternoon, the students gather in hordes on the debate ground and the game starts.

Today it is Tsering Norbu's turn to take the role of the challenger and his friend Yeshe is the defender. According to tradition, Yeshe sits on the ground with Tsering standing in front of him: "If something is a cause, it cannot be an effect."

Bringing forward his proposition, he stretches out his arms and claps his hands, not only to open up the defender's mind, but as a symbol for mind and intuition working together, as well. Immediately following this, Tsering turns his left hand down, the right hand up, and stamps one foot firmly on the ground at the same time. This gesture also has a meaning: the wish to liberate all beings from the cycle of existences, which is full of suffering, by means of wisdom power.

In answer to Tsering's challenge Yeshe counters promptly: "But taking for example something which has an effect, this is not necessarily an effect, is it?"

And again Tsering claps his hands: "Why not?"

"Because it is a cause," the answer comes promptly.

Very soon other students enter into the debate. "Just because it is a cause, does not mean it cannot be an effect."

The argument goes back and forth for a long time. Eventually, bystanders take pleasure in loudly commenting and contributing to the questions and answers. To enforce one's own argument or to undermine the opponent's sense of security, students even use methods which are not quite proper. Besides a piercing gaze or raising one's eyebrows, these tactics also include shoving and pushing or pulling the opponent by his robes. It is not necessarily the objective to bring a debate to a logical conclusion during one session. Depending on how

complex the topic is, it can continue for days, weeks, or months.

The origin of logical debate goes back to the Tibetan Lama Chapa Chokyi Senge, who composed the first textbook on the art of debate in the 12th century. Chapa's tradition has been further developed throughout the centuries, and until today it has been an essential part of the monastic education system. Texts and scriptures of Tibetan Buddhism, which are intensively studied and memorized, serve as the basis; for monks and nuns should be able to come forward with the various philosophical positions – promptly and in a sequence of arguments – in order to defend the respective view in a clear and logical way. It may take between 15 and 25 years of studies before taking the final exams, which includes the demonstration of the candidate's abilities during a debate. Basically the objective of debate is to gain knowledge for the purpose of one's spiritual development. This includes the ability to show and validly prove one's debating opponent that he is deluded. Otherwise he would be stuck in his erroneous views. Building on delusion, however, it is impossible for a higher consciousness to develop.

The first and most important step is to prove the law of cause and effect. According to the Buddhist theory of Valid Cognition, the idea that causes and effects are permanent is false. If they were, the only conclusion left would be that all that exists was permanent by nature and that the idea of a permanent self could not be abandoned; but our existence is impermanent, so this is what has to be proven.

Left: An afternoon of debate at Drepung Monastery, South India.
Right: Monks debating at the entrance to Sera Monastery in South India, in preparation of an exam; a teacher attentively listening to his student's arguments; two monks engaged in 'persuading' the defender; from the viewpoint of the defender; sometimes an argument is incomprehensible.

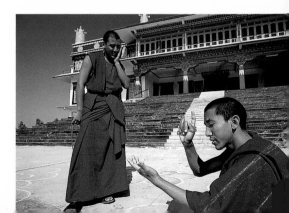

DHARAMSALA

March 23, 2003, Dharamsala, India

"Do you need a candle?" asks Ngawang Mothup, an elderly monk. Monks and nuns, young and old stand close together, each of them carrying a candle in his hands, with rapt attention and looking deeply moved.

I walk the kora with 2,000 others in Dharamsala late at night as if in a sea of light. Dolma, a nun from Sikkim, hand in hand with her grandmother, smiles and shouts, "People shouldn't be passive."

This peace march together with the spirituality of the place is overwhelming. I can feel people's power and hope. With devotion in their hearts they murmur or chant the mantra of Avalokiteshvara, the Bodhisattva of compassion, "Om mani padme hum."

Words of the Dalai Lama appear in my mind.

Earlier today in his teaching, he spoke about compassion – a fundamental virtue in Buddhist ethics, a key notion of Tibetan Buddhism.

"In tse-wa, the Tibetan word for compassionate love, there is an underlying sense of wishing well for oneself. For a start, there is no objection to nourishing this emotion for one's own sake and the wish to be free of suffering. Eventually, we can cultivate that feeling, let it grow and expand toward the outer world and include others."

The peace march comes to an end.

Tomorrow the teachings of the Dalai Lama will continue. I am looking forward to that.

Countless people have gathered in the large open space in front of the Namgyal Monastery prayer hall in the morning, many of them having come from far away places to attend the ten-day teachings of the Dalai Lama. Among the monks and nuns in their dark-red robes there are visitors from Ladakh and Zanskar, who are recognizable to me because of their traditional attires. The atmosphere is peaceful in spite of the large congregation. Everybody listens intently to the words of the Dalai Lama, who speaks to us for five hours each day, without a break. Some have pen and paper to jot down every word he says. I can identify further familiar faces, some from the West. Yesterday, during the peace march I saw the French monk and photographer Matthieu Ricard, whose words I can clearly remember:

We live in a world of perceptions that we confuse with reality.

All eyes are directed toward the Dalai Lama. Calmly, but nonetheless powerfully, he talks about the need to realize one's mental and spiritual life as the true and stable basis for attaining authentic happiness and peace.

Even ten days later I cannot make out more than a few who are tired from listening. On the contrary, I can see bright eyes full of hope.

The Dalai Lama finishes his talk with these words:

"We are surrounded by precious and rare opportunities and we should recognize their value, for we have attained the precious attributes of human life and we should not waste it uselessly. We should rather take advantage of it in a meaningful way and follow the Dharma, the universal law, which is the law of love and compassion."

On the last day of the teachings, I have an interview with His Holiness. In private audience I recount my search for the Golden Tara.

Smilingly he wishes me good luck. "The best you can do is to tell as many individuals as possible what you have seen. This way, more and more people in the world will get to know about the tragedy of Tibet." With the blessing of the Dalai Lama, the next step of my journey takes me to Nepal. I will try to find Pasang Lama.

Interview with His Holiness the 14th Dalai Lama

Dieter Glogowski: Is there a common message in all world religions?

Dalai Lama: Although all the great traditions have different philosophies and their own message, the essence of all traditions is more or less the same. And this message is: love, compassion, forgiveness, tolerance, patience, contentment and self-discipline. This message is inherent in all traditions.

Dieter Glogowski: It is thus the basis of good qualities, isn't it?

Dalai Lama: Yes! I believe that these human qualities are fundamental and that they are good. The purpose of these qualities is to strengthen people. Here strength is not referred to in terms of physical strength but in relation to consciousness. People who have such qualities experience calmness and peace. Their mind cannot be affected by negative influences from the outside. Negative emotions like hatred, jealousy, or anger will not proliferate when one's basic frame of mind is calm and peaceful.

Therefore these qualities are called 'good qualities.' We strive for a happy and successful life. Precisely for this reason, these good qualities are important factors for our contentment. Some say there is a creator, a god who represents the absolute. Jesus is the creator who loves us.

Therefore, if we truly love God, we will have true love for our fellow human beings, as well. For, basically, we are all brothers and sisters, we all have the same origin.

If we really love and seriously respect God, this true love and respect should become visible in our daily life. Of course we cannot communicate directly with God, but we can communicate with our fellow human beings, with our brothers and sisters. We should show our true love and our compassion toward our fellow human beings. This is, in my opinion, the greatest gift, the greatest offering to God.

Dieter Glogowski: This seems to be the root of the common message.

Dalai Lama: Exactly! So we can see that different traditions have different philosophies, but they all have the same common objective, a common message, a similar method. There are different philosophies because practical approaches are different. This is the reason for the variety of philosophies, it corresponds to the differences in human existence.

The gospel, for example, is very similar to the Buddhist teachings.

Whether we accept the religions or not, depends on everybody individually. But once we have accepted religious practice, we should really take it seriously. We should try to apply the teaching in our own traditions. It has to be practiced in everyday life.

This way one will attain authentic and inner benefit. Whether a Christian, Buddhist, Hindu, or Muslim, it doesn't matter as long as one is a serious practitioner of one's own tradition. Eventually, by means of that not only individual happiness but also happiness within the social community can be found, that's what I think.

My opinion is that we should at least make a small contribution toward the improvement of society and toward humanity.

Dieter Glogowski: After the takeover of Tibet by the Chinese, the Christian world came into closer and closer contact with the notions of the Buddhist teachings. What can they learn from each other?

Dalai Lama: In spite of my small experience I am convinced that both religious traditions can learn from each other – Buddhists from Christians and vice versa.

Christians could, for example, learn from important Buddhist methods, like the 'law of impermanence.' There are many common features in both traditions. Christian nuns, first in line Mother Teresa, have found a very practical approach.

Generally, Christian congregations make a great contribution toward social welfare. Just think of the many health posts and social facilities in the Tibetan camps in South India which are managed by Christian missions. Here, help is provided for the poor, the sick and the old. This is a wonderful thing, a good example for Buddhist nuns and monks.

These days, it is of great advantage that it is very easy for people to learn from other cultures and traditions. We should make good use of that.

श्लॹ'ඖ'ॹষॹ'ॹষॹ'ॹষॹ

Resistance – Interview with the Monk Bagdro

Dieter Glogowski: Badgro, you were a monk in Ganden, weren't you?

Bagdro: I was young and I was under the influence of Chinese propaganda against the Dalai Lama which was spreading lies about Tibet's history. Two American tourists secretly slipped me a book of His Holiness; so I wanted to learn more about the Tibetan traditions and about Buddhism. Later I took part in protest marches for a 'Free Tibet' because I knew that Tibet was our country, but the Chinese wouldn't accept that by any means.

Dieter Glogowski: That was in March 1988, wasn't it?

Bagdro: Yes, that was on March 5, 1988, during the protest action for a free Tibet. I was among the leaders. Many Tibetans had gathered for this non-violent protest march. But the Chinese immediately opened fire at the demonstrators. Next to me a Tibetan lady was directly hit in the heart, in front of me a little girl died from a bullet in the head. Many demonstrators were kicked or beaten on their heads with rifles.

Young monks were hiding on the monastery roof. Chinese soldiers seized many of them and simply pushed them down into the monastery yard. Most of them did not survive. Myself, I was shot in the leg. Actually, I was able to reach home, but later the police came and arrested me.

Dieter Glogowski: What was happening then at prison?

Bagdro: I was beaten with shotgun butts on the head. Covered in blood, I was questioned, "You want a free Tibet? Here you have your free Tibet!" And they continued the beating. There

were trees in the yard. I was fixed to one of them by the hands, stripped of my clothes, and then they launched their attack. They sneered, "Today there is no Dalai Lama to help you. Today you are alone." And they went on, "We'll show you a free Tibetan house!" and dragged me into a prison cell. On the way I saw many others all over the place who had been hanged on the walls, I saw their wounds from the beatings and the torture. Many of those were pleading with me, "Please, help me, help me!" Others were requesting, "Please, make me die!" They were showing me more prisoners with blood stained faces and sneered, "Look at them, they are all happy Tibetans on a picnic!" For the night they hanged me on the wall and continued the torture. In the morning I was to answer their questions. If I answered correctly, I would be released, they said, if not, I was to be executed. They asked how much the Dalai Lama was paying me and who else was co-operating with me. I said that I didn't receive any money from anybody. I didn't give them any names. They accused me of lying and put electric shock devices in my ears and mouth, they beat me with iron bars, it was hurting like hell. During other nights, I was left lying without clothes, it was bitter cold. They poured water over me, put my feet into ice for more than an hour and then beat them up. The torture went on and on, it was unbearable. The process continued for more than six months. There was scarcely any food, I drank my urine, I ate my jacket. All was full of dirt. Once somebody came and threw bread in the toilet, then another one came to complain how evil we Tibetans were to throw bread in the toilet, scooped it up again together

with the feces and the urine and made us eat it as our soup. Who wouldn't eat it was beaten up. Thereupon I went out of my mind.

Dieter Glogowski: You were released after three years, weren't you?

Bagdro: The Chinese thought that before long I would die from the effects of the torture anyway. I weighed a mere 39 kilograms, had some broken ribs and my mind was completely confused. Friends helped me to escape to India. From there I was brought to a clinic in Paris. After I had recovered somehow I went to Dharamsala.

Dieter Glogowski: There you had your first audience with the Dalai Lama.

Bagdro: In 1991, on the occasion of a special audience, I met his Holiness the 14th Dalai Lama for the first time. When he saw my body he asked what had happened. Other monks were recounting my fate to him. He was thoroughly dismayed. Thereupon we were talking to each other for hours. He wanted to know what they had done to me and to the others in

prison. I informed him of the demonstrations and the subsequent events in prison. Then His Holiness spoke to me about non-violence for two hours. It seemed like a dream. At times I was so overwhelmed that I couldn't stop weeping, I was at a loss with words. The Dalai Lama came over, took my hand, caressed me and kept repeating countless times these words: "Peace is stronger than hate, peace is stronger than violence!"

The Wheel of Life

By Katharina Sommer

Pasang Dorje had hardly realized the seasons changing. Weeks and months, nearly for a whole year, he was occupied many hours per day painting thousands of colored spots onto a large picture. Religious painting is, nevertheless, more than applying paint with a brush. The art of religious painting is connected to blessing rituals, offerings, meditations and prayer; nothing is left the mere chance. Also Pasang's work, the picture of the wheel of life, will not just be a masterpiece when it is finished – it will be a symbol of the Buddhist view, a representation of the meaning of living and dying, and an explanation of the Buddha's teaching.

The original shape of the mandala wheel in Tibetan Buddhism is attributed to Buddha Shakyamuni himself. It is said that the realms of existence, including that of humans beings, the origin of suffering as well as the chain of dependent origination and ceasing, were rendered in the form of a diagram by the Buddha, assisted by his disciples Ananda and Maudgalyayana, in order to make these topics easier comprehensible. Since then this diagram has been reproduced again and again in the form of thangkas or murals, which can be seen in most monasteries, because the symbolic pictures in the wheel teach and admonish observers at the same time.

As a wheel moves from the hub, the innermost circle symbolizes by means of joined up animals the three fundamental characteristics which delude consciousness, produce much ensuing suffering and, yet, are so typical for human beings: the pig stands for ignorance and dullness, the snake for envy and hatred, the cock for greed and covetousness. The background of the next circle is divided by color. Black represents the realm of shades, disastrous reincarnations; but white is the realm of light, which is attained by virtue of positive action. The next circle is divided into six segments illustrating six realms. One of these alone, several, or all of them together have influence on human life. Samsara, the endless cycle of dying and being reborn, is illustrated by means of hell-beings, hungry ghosts, animals, demi-gods, gods and human beings. The wheel turns and as long as one is under the power of the painful emotions of these realms, one will

return there all over again. They who find themselves in the hell-realm because of anger and hatred must endure the inexpressible torment of extreme heat or cold, with poisonous animals lurking everywhere. Hungry ghosts are never satisfied because their craving for wealth and their emotional desires are irrational and impossible to quench. Ignorance, lack of willpower, and a passive daily routine lead to the animal realm. Even though the picture suggests harmony and peace, the danger to end up as a work animal, in a test laboratory or as food is permanently present and creates fear and terror. The realm of the demigods is for the greedy, who are consumed with envy when looking at others' possessions, power and happiness. This is the cause of competition, fighting, intrigue and hostility. The gods, on the other hand, indulge in paradise. Without any effort, they live in the lap of luxury. Nevertheless, they are caught in samsara and – also a god's life is not endless. The human segment is characterized by the sufferings of birth, sickness, old age and death, but also by pleasures. Only from here is it possible to leave the cycle of existences, to reach liberation. The metaphor is a small bridge leading to a white temple symbolizing nirvana, the absolute freedom from any worldly manifestation. The outer circle shows twelve allegories describing the chain of interdependent origination. The giant demon holding the wheel firmly in its claws cannot be identified without doubt. Pasang, although very familiar with the complex iconography of Tibetan Buddhism, is not sure if here we see Yama, the Lord of Death, or Mara, the Buddha's tempter.

Left: A wonderful depiction of the wheel of life can be admired at Paro Dzong in Bhutan.
Right: The six realms of existence in the wheel of life (from above): the world of gods and demi-gods, the world of human beings, the animal world, the world of hungry ghosts, the world of Yama, the Lord of Death, who puts one's former actions on the weighing scales and makes his judgment.

NEPAL

August 3, 2003, Kathmandu, Nepal

I find peace and strength at Swayambhunath. This religious site is one of the oldest in the Kathmandu Valley. Situated on a hill with a wide view over the valley, it is a place of contemplation and calmness, a place where Buddhism and Hinduism unite. Here many symbols and elements of both religions are woven into each other. In the same way, the belief of the Sakya-Newari living in the valley is a combination of these two lines of thought.

Even though Swayambhunath is a very special place of calmness and inner rest, my thoughts keep wandering to Pasang Lama. Maybe I will find him in his home monastery Melamchighyang, a small settlement in the Helambu Langtang region.

I want to ask my friend Rade-Baba to accompany me on my way to Melamchighyang via the holy lakes of Gosainkund. Hundreds of shamans will meet there for the full-moon night of August to celebrate the Hindu festival Janai Purnima. It was five years ago when I met Rade-Baba at the temple of Pashupatinath for the first time. He told me his life story and how he had decided to become a Sadhu when he was 20. Injustice, discord and selfishness among people had weighed upon his mind; he was searching for a life of peace and ease, free from material desires. Having roamed about for a long time, he had come to Pashupatinath in the Kathmandu Valley. Once upon a time, the God Shiva had dwelled there with his wife Parvati. For Rade-Baba it is a place of refuge.

The night before we are to set off, rain is coming down in torrents. The mud road, sodden with rain, has become a single sliding track. We are to climb 2,500 meters (8,200 feet) higher. Torrential waters thunder downhill, dense swathes of mist chase uphill, deep green forests, fog and silence – all seems to be touched by a magical spell. Dozens of leeches creep into our shoes, find there way up, attach themselves to the skin, and let us bleed. After a climb of seven hours, we rest in Shingompa.

Rade-Baba is talking about desires and wishes while I reflect on the words of Kalu Rinpoche:

Craving for possessions results in deprivation, non-attachment results in contentment.

Except for a water bowl, a blanket and a small bundle of clothes, Rade-Baba is weighed down by nothing. We continue to Gosainkund. The holy lakes spread out before us at an altitude of 4,381 meters (14,370 feet). Like a sheet of glass they reflect the emerald green mountain slopes. The night before, Rade-Baba immediately went to worship the phallic symbol of Shiva, the God of destruction and revival. Silently Rade whispered the mantra "Om namah Shivaya" – in the name of Shiva, who destroys all ignorance. He is the father of love, the ruler of the God realm.

August 12, 2003, Gosainkund, Nepal

The night is cold, rain drops keep hammering on the tent roof incessantly. The sounds of drums and rattles rouse me from my dreams. It is not even six in the morning; the Hindu festival Janai Purnima is beginning. Still in darkness hundreds of shamans, Sadhus and Nepali pilgrims have arrived at the holy site in spite of the heavy monsoon rains.

Every village of the region had sent their own shaman, accompanied by a crowd of villagers. Some protect themselves from the torrents with umbrellas or plastic sheets. Others are simply dripping wet. Obliviously, the shamans are beating the big incantation drums with their wooden beaters. Many are wearing the same dresses: robes hung with bells and cymbals, white skirts, and turbans.

Drums, magical chants, and dance rituals bring about a mystical spell-bound atmosphere. All of them set off to circumambulate the lake. They pacify the Gods. Shamans wade in the ice
cold crystal clear water, showing their devotion to Shiva. As the
legend goes, Shiva himself created the lakes by knocking his
trident into the rock. From the very spot fresh water bubbled
out and he could quench his thirst.

The following morning, at daybreak, we start out toward the south east. There is a long way to go; and at first this means climbing! We cross the Laura-Bina pass, which is 4,509 meters (14,790 feet) high. Two days later in the late evening, while sheets of monsoon rain are coming down, we arrive in Melam-

Kami is kind enough to show us to the small gompa where the masks are kept. The door opens with a creak. The dusty masks leaning on the walls, have fierce, wrathful expressions, some are centuries old. One, baring its teeth, wears a garland of four skulls on the forehead – a symbol of impermanence. "Bhutan?"

chighyang. The shape of the old monastery is hardly visible. The narrow streets are deserted.

In our lodge we ask for Pasang Lama and are sent to his elder sister Kami.

"Pasang Lama?"

Kami gives me a questioning look. "Well, many years ago he went to Bhutan. His last message came from Wangdi Dzong. He went to study the art of masked dancing. But that was more than 20 years ago!"

In Melamchighyang ritual masked dance has a long tradition, as well. The precious colorful masks represent gods and demons and are never shown except at specific mystery plays and devotional dances.

I inquire once more. The journey will continue, it seems. Did I fancifully believe I would solve Tara's secret in the first go? Sogyal Rinpoche would say, "Get free from concepts." Also, I remember Dilgo Khyentse Rinpoche:

Our mind, our mind alone, is what binds us or what liberates us

Once he even went on to say: "Western people eat concepts" and roared with laughter. Smiling to myself, I make preparations for the trip to the land of the thunder dragon.

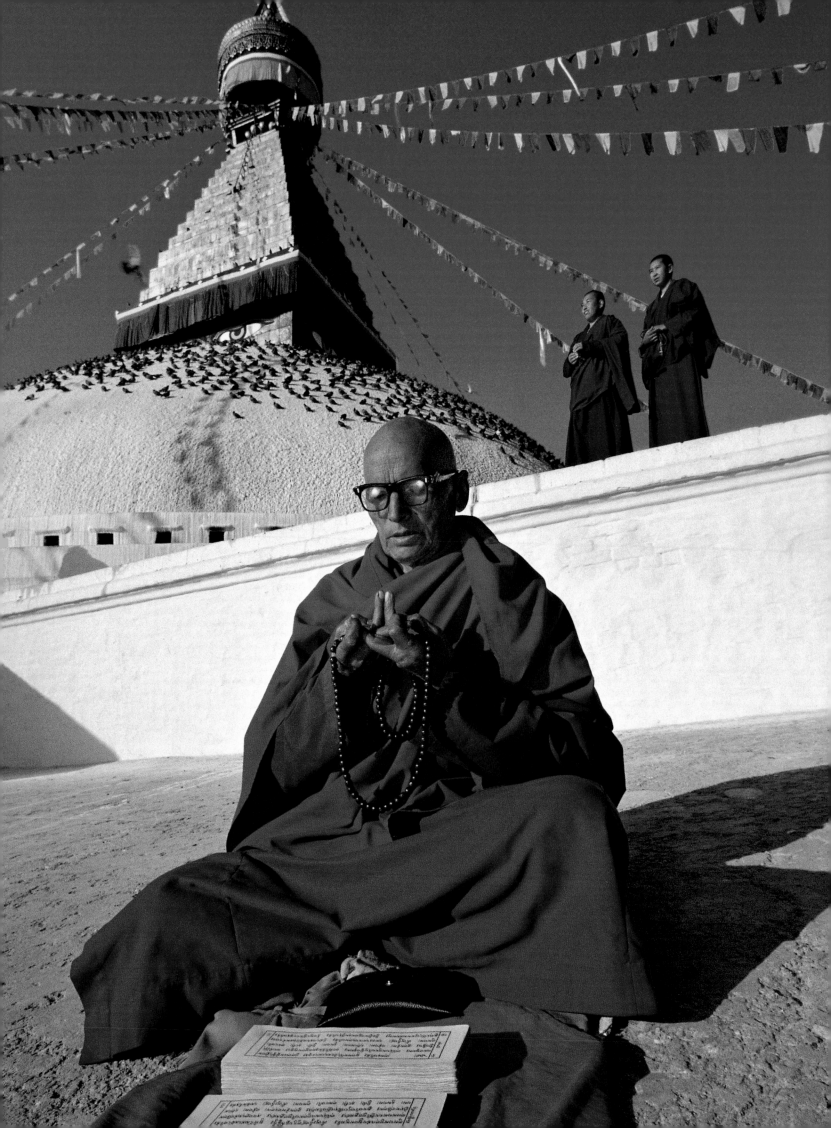

The Great Stupa of Boudhanath
By Katharina Sommer

"In heaven, Apurna, one of God Indra's daughters, once had stolen flowers for her hair. As a punishment she was sent to the human realm." Dolma listens to her father Lobsang Donyo's stories with eyes wide open. He knows lots of legends about the origin of the Great Stupa. "In the family of a chicken dealer, as their daughter Shamvara, Apurna had a good life," he continues. "All her striving on earth was directed toward having a stupa constructed as a means of support for the mind of all the Buddhas, a shrine for the relics of the Thus-Gone-One Mahakashyapa, the Buddha of the previous era. Thus she related her plans to the Maharaja of the country, who was impressed by her idea and promised her a piece of land for the purpose. But many others did not agree with the project and tried to stop it. 'Wasn't it an insult to the Maharaja,' they argued, 'if a simple woman like her could accomplish such a spectacular plan? How could any ruler ever be able to surpass such a project?' But –," Lobsang smiles to himself, "– the Maharaja could not be persuaded to change his mind. Thus the stupa received its name Jarung Khashor – permission once given – already in the initial stages of its construction. As is said, Shamvara reached Buddhahood already while the stupa was still under construction, and she left her body before the site was consecrated, meaning that the stupa was brought to life by means of the spirit and power of millions of Buddhas, Bodhisattvas and Arhats. Her four sons completed the work."

The Great Stupa of Boudhanath is 40 meters (131 feet) high and the largest construction of its kind. Since 1959, it has been the main pilgrimage site outside of Tibet for all Tibetans in exile. Scientifically it cannot be verified when exactly it was built. In all four schools of Tibetan Buddhism the stupa is equally revered as a symbol of enlightened mind, as a symbol of the whole universe, and as a symbol of the basic elements. The stupa is a three-dimensional mandala with architecture highly symbolic on many different levels. When compared to the nine levels of Mount Kailash, the mystical center of the universe, the base of the stupa is considered to be a symbol of the underworld. The three-story terraces with their twice retracted corners represent our world. The huge

hemisphere, eventually, symbolizes the world of the Gods; it has a square tower on top, which gets narrower with each of its thirteen-steps and is crowned by a parasol. From the foundations of the upper tower the eyes of the Buddha gaze into all four directions; the numeral one between them represents the one and only path to enlightenment. As representations of the basic elements, the terraced foundation is related to the earth element, the hemisphere to the water element, the tower to the fire element, and the parasol to the element of space. The very top relates to the sphere of clear mind. The perimeter of the site is a huge wall with 147 recesses for prayer wheels. At the base of the hemisphere there are 108 openings, each enshrining a manifestation of the Bodhisattva Avalokiteshvara. Other than Dolma and Lobsang, who live only 8 kilometers (5 miles) away in Kathmandu, many Tibetans in exile bear with the hardship of many days of pilgrimage to receive the positive energy of the holy site in Boudhanath. Because they who come to circumambulate the stupa respectfully in contemplative absorption and with a good heart, or pay homage by means of prostration, will discover that their prayers for mental development and realization will be fulfilled. As the legend goes, the noble master Padmasambhava, who introduced Buddhism to Tibet in the 8th century, has described the stupa as a wish-fulfilling jewel. Padmasambhava's explanations about the Great Stupa are written down in an old Tibetan scripture which was twice hidden as a terma in order to be rediscovered at the right moment. The text contains teachings for the spiritual path as well as prophecies on Tibet's fate, which partly have come true already.

Left: In the early morning hours – the hand gesture of the mandala offering shown by a monk in Boudhanath, the center for Tibetans in Nepal.
Right: Butter lamps illuminate the stupa during the Saga Dawa festival; monks call for a special ceremony with their long radongs; young monks having fun during their afternoon circumambulation of the stupa; Buddha's eyes are omnipresent.

The source of happiness is a compassionate and loving heart.
From the moment onward that one enters into this world,
one longs for happiness and intuitively tries to avoid suffering,
no matter what social level one was born into,
which education one has received, which ideology one has grown up with,
or in which country one has lived.
I do not know about any superior political system, but everyone should,
nevertheless, have a right to be happy in his own country.

THE 14TH DALAI LAMA

BHUTAN

October 2, 2003, Bhutan

"He came flying here on a tiger. How else could he have reached here? The cave is in the middle of that vertical granite rock, and the gorge is 400 meters (1,300 feet) deep." Tenzing's eyes are shining. "He came as Dorje Drolo in one of his wrathful appearances – he must have looked really fearsome. He meditated here for four months, after that all the local gods, spirits and demons were subdued."

The view is incredible. At a distance of only 200 meters (656 feet) I can see the most famous monastery of the whole Himalayan region at eye-level – Taktsang Monastery, the Tiger's Nest. Tenzing talks about the great Indian Guru Padmasambhava, the originator of the Nyingma tradition. "All over the steep rock walls he had hidden termas. They are scriptures meant for future times. Over the centuries, now and then, some have been discovered by tertons, the treasure finders. Presumably, nowhere near all of these secret texts have been recovered in this mountain region. Milarepa and the 1st Karmapa were here, as well."

Tenzing sits next to me in the grass. All my life I have dreamed of coming to this place one day. The Tiger's Nest is the most powerful place in Bhutan, countless myths and legends are connected to it. The mask dances which Ngawang Namgyal Shabrung Rinpoche, the founder of the kingdom, is said to have compiled at this holy place have been celebrated until today. After three days, the dance festival in Wangdi Dzong will begin.

October 5, 2003, Wangdi Dzong

Seeing Wangdi Dzong, I am not at all surprised that Bhutan has never been occupied by a foreign power. Strategically well placed, it towers above the mountaintop, invincible. As a fortress, castle monastery and administrative seat it is a home for about 2,000 monks and lay people with religious and worldly functions. Before the construction of the first roads in the nineteen sixties, the Dzongs, which are spread throughout the country, could be reached only on foot paths which were difficult to travel.

Reaching the entrance of the Dzong via a steep wooden staircase, we pass through its six-meter thick (20 feet) outer walls. The sound of cymbals and drums is increasing. In the yard hundreds of monks and well over a thousand other spectators watch the mask dances. Buddha's words come to my mind:

Having rehearsed for months, monks and lay people here perform the victory of the Dharma. Dressed in heavy brocade robes, huge wooden masks on their heads, they whirl across the monastery yard to show the audience the game of life and death and rebirth. At night, after the dances, I start looking for Pasang. "Pasang Lama? The monk from Nepal? He is no longer here. Ask Namgyal Lama! He was a close friend of his, maybe he can help you," is the advice I get from the ceremonial master of Wangdi Dzong. "Namgyal lives at Tongza Dzong. Maybe you will find him there!"

Five days later I reach the monastic fortress of Tongza. "Namgyal went into retreat nine month ago. He is in meditation and stays in a small hermitage in the mountains. After three more months, his retreat will be finished and he is to become the discipline master in Phunaka Dzong. There you can meet him."

This existence of ours is as transient as autumn clouds.
To watch the birth and death of beings is like looking at the movements of a dance.

A lifetime is like a flash of lightning in the sky, rushing by, like a torrent down a steep mountain.

The old gatekeeper of the temple turns his back on me and leaves.

February 28, 2004, Phunaka Dzong

Hundreds of warriors in historical costumes are lined up in Phunaka Dzong. Here, every year in spring time, they perform a play in memory of a military stratagem that occurred in the 17th century.

For the third time Tibetan troops invaded Bhutan to gain recovery of a small statue of Avalokiteshvara which Ngawang Namgyal Shabrung, the founder of the kingdom, had taken with him on his escape from Tibet. The Tibetans wanted it back because it is said, after all, to have grown from the cervical vertebra of their first king Songtsen Gampo. As it was, the Tibetan troops were besieging Phunaka, so a battle seemed inevitable. But before it came to fighting, the two sides were negotiating by the river banks. Ngawang had brought the statue and declared that it did not belong to anybody. With his arm outstretched, he held it over the water. But before hurling it into the river he let it fall in a long sleeve turn-up of his robe and instead he hurled a duplicate into the water. The Tibetans were satisfied and withdrew. By means of this trick, blood shed was prevented. As Pema Chödrön says:

uffering is part of human experience.
eople keep hurting each other –
e hurt others and others hurt us.
o know is to have a clear view.

This battle which was, eventually, not fought is celebrated for four days in Phunaka Dzong every spring. The soldiers allow themselves to do as they please, exuberantly they roam the Dzong, and chang, the traditional brew, flows freely. Gunfire rumbles, trumpets sound, there is dancing and roaring, women are scared, particularly because a red warrior's cap can easily be formed into a penis – a ritual which in times of war was meant to provoke the opponents. In Bhutan the image of penises can be found on nearly every house wall. If painted or carved in the roof ledge, not only do they symbolize fertility, they also avert demons.

On the last day of the festival, the Je Khenpo, the most senior monk in Bhutan, goes once again to the river bank and pours a bowl of fruits into the floods – as a symbol for the stratagem of ancient times.

One day after the festival, I roam the Dzong and discover the picture of the late King Jigme Dorje Wangchuck in a small shrine room. Clever and wise, he lead Bhutan out of century-long isolation and connected traditional Buddhist values with the influence of modernity from the Western world of the 20th century. I remain for a long time and contemplate the Dalai Lama's words:

It is Karma Namgyal, the newly elected ceremonial master of Phunaka Dzong. He gazes at my amulet.

"Yes, I have seen this amulet. Pasang Lama was my close and good friend. 14 years ago, at the time when our government banished thousands of illegal Nepali immigrants from the country, Pasang Lama also went away. As far as I know, he lives in Sikkim now, not far from Rumtek Monastery. In Rumtek you

If we direct our lives toward compassion and altruism, then we will be able to achieve great accomplishments.

He continues: "If we succeed to use our lives in a constructive way, this will be meaningful in a long-term perspective. Then our lives will be really precious."

can ask for a lay monk by the name of Sangay Temba. Pasang had left with him. The two monks were friends. I'm sure he can help you with what he knows." So I decide to leave Bhutan.

"You want to talk to me?" a deep voice asks me from behind. I turn around and before me there is a bald-headed monk. His features are solemn, his eyes mild and wise.

Twice I have visited this wonderful country with its unique features. Above all, I have grown fond of the people because I also appreciate the values they hold.

Dance and Miracle Play
By Franz Binder

Cham dance and miracle play are the highlights of the year in many monasteries of the Tibetan cultural tradition. But nowhere else are these monastic celebrations as magnificent and diverse as in Bhutan, the Buddhist 'Kingdom of the Thunder Dragon' in the South Eastern Himalaya. Whereas such dance and miracle plays are limited to religious contents in Tibet and other places which are influenced by Tibetan culture, in Bhutan in addition to that they also comprise ethnic dance, spiritual drama and the like. Such worldly parts of the monastic festivals are performed by lay people, whereas religious dance is a privilege of monks and lamas only.

The performances have different symbolic and religious levels of meaning. Traditionally, dance and miracle play were to serve the purpose of bringing home the basic points of the Buddhist teachings to the people who were not able to read nor write, and illustrate to them the workings of superior powers subduing the constant threat of demonic forces. The religious plays are more than just teaching by means of dance, symbolic demon fighting, and illustrating the life stories of saints and yogis. They also directly invoke the activity and energy of spiritual beings, help to remove obstacles and disruption on the path to enlightenment, and they allow even the non-initiate to experience the blessing of the performing deities. The 'human element' is also satisfied, mainly by the Atsaras, the jokers, who counterbalance the serious sacredness of the religious plays. To the great enjoyment of the spectators, they interfere in the performance with their rough and obscene jokes, without ever going beyond the limit of what is tolerable. They provide the outlet for the release of the atmosphere, intensified by the magical events; and by means of their commentary and jokes they make the contents and symbolic meaning of the performance accessible to the audience. The incomparable atmosphere of these monastic festivals is characterized by the natural coexistence of the spiritual and the worldly, of seriousness and fun, of devoted faith and carefree joy.

The dances are supported by the musical instruments which are normally played in the monastic ceremonies. Ritual music provides the rhythm for the dance and the background for

the events on the dance floor. On top of that it serves to distract adverse energies and to actually invite the deities and demons which are represented by the performers.

The subject of many dances is the overcoming, banning, and sometimes even killing of demons, as well as the transforming of unwholesome powers into positive energies. By means of their 'thunderbolt steps' the dancers crush negative impact underfoot, and by means of spinning, which makes their skirts rotate around them, they indicate that positive powers work every which way. The dancers' costumes, their masks, the colors and the attributes of the deities represented are in accordance with the iconographical rules of Vajrayana Buddhism, which are also valid for the plastic arts.

From among the various dances and magical plays, every monastery makes its own choice and sequence. Black Hat Dance, Dance of the Lord of Graveyards, Dance of the Eight Demons, Dance of the Deer, Dance of Fury, these are just a few of the most common ones. Then there are magical plays, like Judgment of Death; and legends, like the Story of Milarepa, the Deer and the Hunter. The absolute highlight of many monastic festivals is the appearance of Padmasambhava's eight manifestations. People in long cues push and shove to receive the blessing of Guru Rinpoche, because they are certain that on this occasion Padmasambhava is truly present in their midst.

Many monastic festivals end with a ceremonial act. In the early morning hours the monastery's huge thangka is rolled out and displayed either on a certain wall reserved for the purpose or on one of the buildings; then it is ritually purified. At sunrise it is rolled up again and the spectators disperse.

Left and right: Every year in fall, Wangdi Dzong celebrates its mask dance festival.

Real life we experience here and now.
The past has gone, and the future has not yet arrived.
Only in the present moment can we really touch life.

THICH NHAT HANH

SIKKIM

April 22, 2004, Darjeeling, India

The streets of Darjeeling are busy and colorful, noisy and dusty – chaos unique to India. Appreciated since long for its mild climate, the townscape still shows old villas – relics from colonial times. Some of them have lost their charm; others are magnificent as always and give an impression of the once ostentatious British way of life. Darjeeling is the center of Bengali tea cultivation; deep green it nestles for a few kilometers against a downward sloping mountain, embedded in extensive tea plantations and terraced fields interspersed with trees, the only source of shadow. On the horizon the silhouette of the mighty Himalaya mountain range rises. At Druk Sangak Choeling Monastery I find the time and peace to think things over.

"Do you like this painting?" Two little novices come up toward me: "This is the guru of our heart." With laughter they pose in front of the huge painting of Avalokiteshvara, the Buddha of compassion. Some time later, I sit in a shared taxi on the way to Kalimpong. I look out of the window and see the landscape whizzing by.
Words of Buddha Shakyamuni occupy my mind. Didn't he say one should rely on the message of one's teacher and not on his personality, not on his words alone or on the meaning of his words, but only on the ultimate meaning, not the provisional? He also said one should rely on one's wisdom mind and not on one's ordinary mind.

I can recognize the snow-covered peak of the 8,586-meter-high (28,162 feet) Kanchendzonga in the North. Entering Sikkim: the four-wheel drive struggles its way up the zigzagging mountain road to Kalimpong with the engine roaring. I stay in a hotel, whose hospitality Alexandra David Néel, Heinrich Harrer and other travelers enjoyed before me. A minor road winds up through a steep mountainous countryside and through rhododendron forests toward Gangtok and Rumtek, Sikkim's largest monastery complex.

Since his escape from his Tibetan home monastery in Tsurphu in the year 2000, the 17th Karmapa has resided in Dharamsala. So far, India has refused to let him re-occupy Rumtek Monastery, which was founded by the 16th Karmapa in 1962.

I enter the monastery gate, pausing at a monk's cell. There is a torn sticker on the window: Karmapa back to Rumtek!

An old man coming out of the room points at it with a serious face: "Yes, it is high time that the Indian authorities give His Holiness the 17th Karmapa permission to come to Rumtek!"

I ask him about Sangay Temba. "You are looking for Old Sangay?" Turning toward me he continues: "He lives at Zangdogpalri Monastery near Kalimpong."

In the yard two young monks, beaming with joy, show me a photograph of their young head lama. They lead me to a wall painting of Tsurphu Monastery. I discover the picture of Ganesha, a Hindu deity with an elephant's head. It is said that Ganesha has appeared to the 16th Karmapa in his dreams and helped him with the construction of the monastery. The 16th Karmapa as the founder of the monastery is highly revered. A big colorful statue shows him in a sitting posture, his hands forming a mudra.

One day later, I reach Zangdogpalri Monastery. The sun is at its zenith, the sky is blue and cloudless. In front of the monastery's Dokhang an old man sits in the half shadow of a wall. He looks at me in surprise, points at the amulet on my neck. "I have seen that before!"

I ask him if he knows Sangay Temba. He nods, "Yes that's me." While I am telling my story, he murmurs, "Pasang Lama is no longer alive." Without another word he gets up and leaves. Is this the end of my search because Pasang Lama is dead? I remember Sogyal Rinpoche's words:

Learning how to live means learning how to let go.

Impermanence is a principle of harmony, thus a Tibetan wisdom word says that farewell is just another name for fresh start, and death is just another name for life.

Whatever you leave behind will re-emerge in another shape. With a small packet wrapped up in cloth, recovered from Pasang Lama's casket, he returns. Reverently he holds it against his forehead. Opening it, an amulet comes forth. It is the same as mine. The yellow cloth turns out to be a prayer flag. At the bottom two words are written in Tibetan letters: 13 Chorten. Eventually, a strange stone emerges. "Dawa, nyima," murmurs Sangay, "moon and sun." The riddle is solved.

Sangay holds the stone with both hands at his chest; for a long time he clasps it to his heart. Then he gives it to me. The surface is very smooth; I follow the light brown pattern with my fingers.

The symbols of the half-moon and the sun are clearly visible. How can a piece of stone create itself in this way? A sun disc on top of a horizontal half-moon is a representation of two

I know but one place in the whole Himalaya region where there are 13 chortens: 6,000 meters (19,680 feet) high at the steep South wall of Mount Kailash at the turning point of the inner kora. Exactly there is where the center of Tibetan cosmology lies: the inner mandala!

I have found the key, my odyssey is over; for the amulet, the prayer flag and the stone tell me that Pasag Lama has fulfilled

sacred places of Tibetan Buddhism: Mount Kailash and Lake Manasarovar in West Tibet.

his task. Most probably he has taken the Tara to the inner kora of Mount Kailash.

Real life we experience here and now. The past has gone, and the future has not yet arrived. Only in the present moment can we really touch life.

Sangay and me, we look at each other for a long time. How true these words of Thich Nhat Hanh are. Sangay's eyes are clear and alert. I feel free – as if I have never had a doubt, as if I have never thought about yesterday or tomorrow.

Next door, a young monk sits deep in meditation. His hands show a three-dimensional mandala, in the middle Mount Meru, the center of the universe, a symbol of the holy Mount Kailash. My journey is certain.

Alexandra David-Néel – Lama Yongden

En souvenir de votre grand-Père David MacDonald
à Tim MacDonald

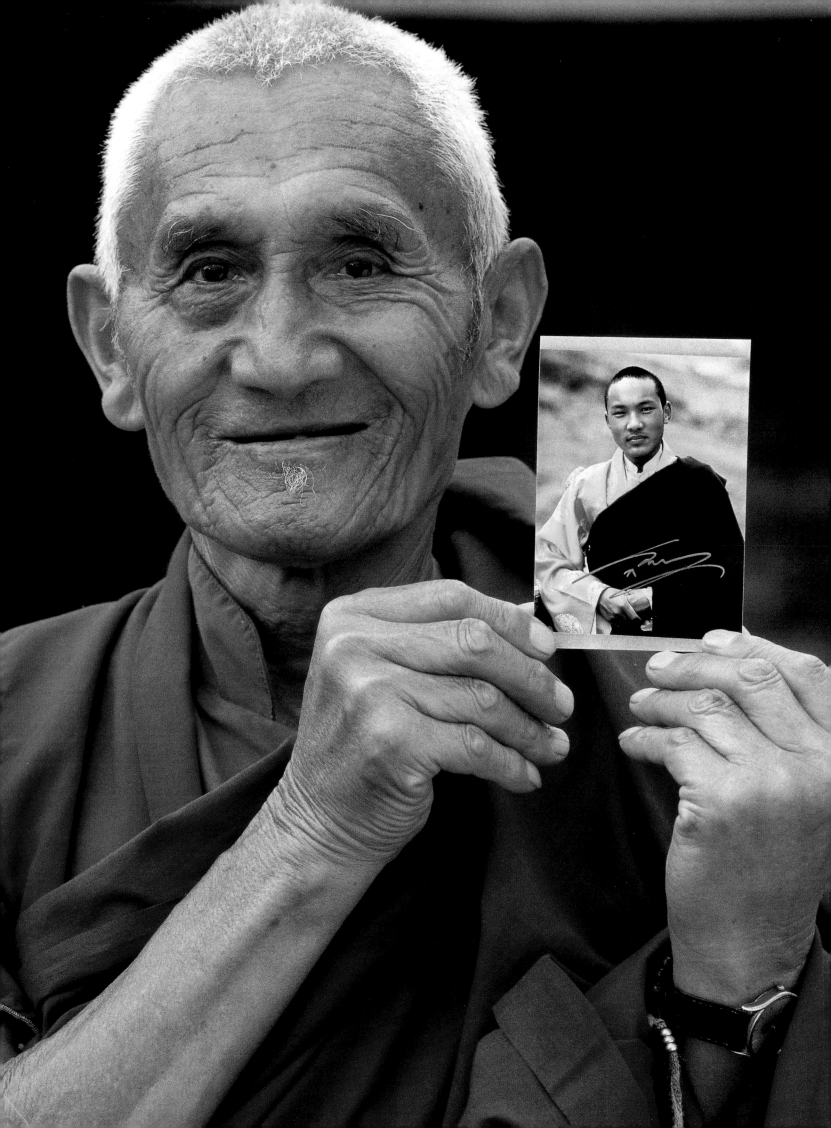

Karmapa – Tibet's Oldest Line of Incarnations
By Klemens Ludwig

In terms of popularity, no one among the Tibetans can measure up to the standard of the Dalai Lama; but in terms of the traditional line of incarnations, the Karmapa is the leading figure in Tibet. The Karmapa is the head of the Kagyu school, one of the four main lines of Tibetan Buddhism. It goes back to Guru Marpa and to Milarepa, two fascinating characters in Tibetan history. Guru Marpa (1012–1090) was the first important local teacher of Buddhism; the ones before him had all come across the Himalaya from India. His disciple Milarepa (1040–1123) was a mystic, yogi and poet, who attained enlightenment within one lifetime after he had been through the hard school of Guru Marpa. Milarepa's major disciple was Gampopa (1079–1153), followed by Dusum Khyenpa (1110–1193), who was the first Karmapa, the 'master of karma.' The Kagyupas were the initiators of the practice of forming a line of reincarnations. The belief in the cycle of rebirths is a fundamental part of Buddhist philosophy; nevertheless, a specific line of incarnations was not commonly cultivated until the 12th century. Introduced by the Kagyupas, spiritual continuity received particular importance and was comparable to family continuity.

Although Dusum Khyenpa had originally resided and worked in East Tibet, in 1189 the main seat of the Kagyupas was founded at Tsurphu, 60 kilometers (37 miles) north west of Lhasa. When the first Karmapa passed away, he left a letter with exact instructions on how to recognize his re-incarnation. This tradition has been kept until today. The political influence of the Kagyupas was gradually limited by the reformed school of the Gelugpas with the Dalai Lama as their head. Politically they reached their final full blossoming under the 9th and 10th Karmapa in the 16th century. At that time the Tsangpa were ruling in Shigatse, who in terms of theology had acknowledged the Kagyupas. In 1642, the Mongols, who were in alliance with the Gelugpas, inflicted a crushing defeat on them. Since then the importance of the Karmapa has been exclusively of spiritual nature. In 1959, during the terror reign of the Chinese, the 16th Karmapa escaped to Rumtek Monastery in Sikkim, which became the Kagyupas' center in exile. At the age of 58, on November 6, 1981, he passed away in Chicago. It was the task of Rumtek Monastery's four regents to search for and to authorize his incarnation. One of the four had died in an automobile accident immediately before the decision, and the remaining three could not agree on any of the candidates. Two of them voted for the 17th Karmapa in Gyalwa Urgyen Thinley Dorje, born June 26, 1985; the third presented his own candidate, Trinley Thaye Dorje, who is a little bit younger. The Dalai Lama was convinced by the vote of the majority and acknowledged Gyalwa Urgyen Thinley as the 17th Karmapa; the Chinese government did the same.

The latter has a special story behind it: Gyalwa Urgyen Thinley is originally from the East Tibetan province Kham, which today is ruled by the Chinese. He received his traditional education at Tsurphu Monastery. It was the hope of the Chinese to have a counterbalance for the exiled Dalai Lama in such a high dignitary. He was allowed more privileges than others; but at the same time they continued their propaganda activities against the Dalai Lama; a strategy which did not have the result they were wishing for. Disregarding the hate campaign against the Dalai Lama, to which the young Karmapa was exposed, in his heart he remained steadfast on the side of the head of all Tibetans. However, he could not bear this inner tension any longer. In the beginning of the year 2000, he escaped to India in a nighttime operation, which had been planned well in advance. To avoid loss of face, the Chinese government declared that the Karmapa had only temporarily gone to India to bring home religious implements. However, for the refugee, the return to his occupied homeland is not a realistic option. In exile, the Karmapa is in close contact with the Dalai Lama. As the supreme authority, he is probably meant to prevent the exile community from growing radicalism after the Dalai Lama passes away, until his new incarnation has been found and installed in office.

Left: A monk in the yard of Rumtek Monastery. Right: His Holiness the 17th Karmapa; wall painting of Tsurphu Monastery in Tibet; leaflets from Rumtek Monastery; young monks with a photograph of the 17th Karmapa.

Tibet will rise again one day,
because suppression has never been successful in the long run.
It is the eternal wish of humankind to live in freedom,
to have one's own thoughts, to experience well-being,
and to lead the life of a human, not of a robot or a slave.
Even if the Chinese leave nothing but ashes in Tibet,
we Tibetans, we firmly believe:
Tibet will rise again as a free country, even if it takes a long time.

THE 14TH DALAI LAMA

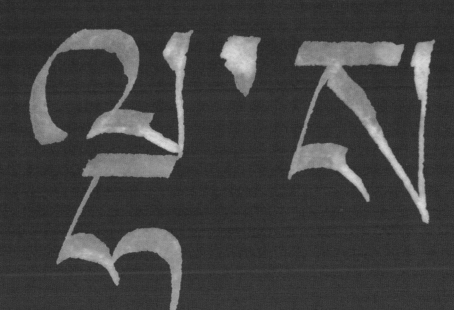

LHASA

June 14, 2004, Lhasa, Tibet

"Nothing is permanent, everything changes. This is the one and only universal law that we Tibetans believe in. I feel the clarity of these wise words, and when I look at Lhasa I feel deep sorrow. My home town has experienced a lot of change under the Chinese." The nun Dawa looks in the direction of the Potala; the first sunrays are touching Lhasa. Continuously she turns her prayer wheel; whilst the mantra of Avalokiteshvara inside rotates a thousand times, as well. Dawa knows that prayers which are activated in this way will spread throughout the entire space for the benefit of all living beings. Countless small scars from burns mark her left arm. There is a long distinguishable scar right across her head. She seems calm and relaxed.

"It happened eight years ago, on the 15th day after Losar, our New Year festival. We met in the late afternoon in front of the Jokhang, because this is the time when many Tibetans come to go kora on the Barkhor, the inner circle around the temple. I filed in line together with 14 other nuns and we were chanting the Tara mantra. Then we pulled out the wooden boards we had brought wrapped in blankets. Written on them were the proclamations 'Free Tibet' and 'Free Panchen Lama.' We shouted 'Chinese out of Tibet' and 'Long live the Dalai Lama.' After a short while, the police came running and began to beat us without any warning. Battered and bleeding we were arrested and taken away. Each of us was sentenced to seven years for what we did."

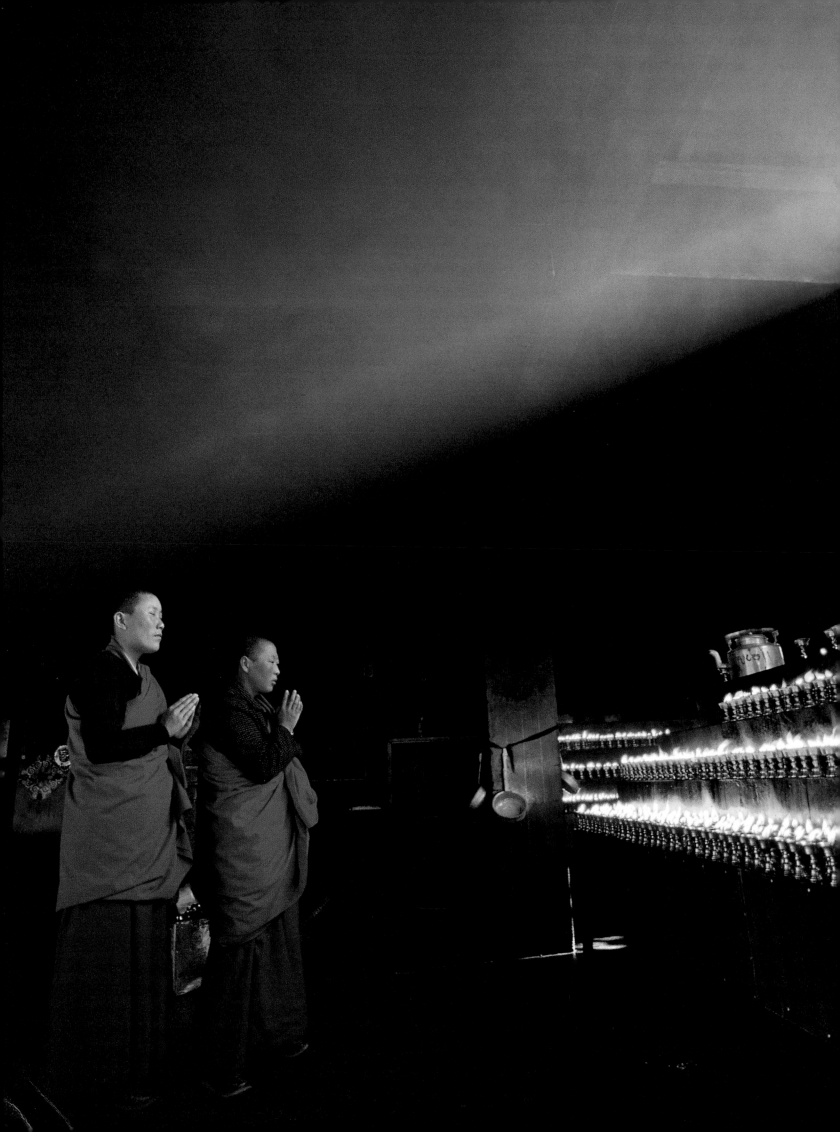

Once more Dawa accompanies me from the Potala to the Jokhang, Lhasa's most sacred place. "Very often we were tortured. They stubbed out cigarettes on my arm; the scar on my head is from an iron bar with which they beat me. But the electric shocks were the worst; we had to be prepared for that each time they questioned us." We enter the room whereupon butter lamps are offered, and there we meet Ani Tsering. The two nuns were in prison together. "We had committed ourselves to compassion toward all sentient beings; eventually, this extends even to our torturers in prison. During the nights, we comforted each other and sang in memory of Shantideva: 'We are not angry with the stick that beats us but with the man who uses it; but this man is governed by hatred. So it is hatred itself we should hate.'" Ani Tsering's words resound in my mind. The nuns have really understood what the Buddha says:

Blessed are those who live without hatred,
although hatred and lack of kindness prevail.
Blessed are those who are not deluded,
although the world is wasting away in delusion.

After all the suffering that the Tibetans had to endure, it is admirable that they have retained their sense of humor and their smile. Once during a retreat, Sogyal Rinpoche was asking: "What does it actually mean to have a sense of humor?" He continued: "A sense of humor is not a giggle and ha, ha, ha after a glass of beer or two. A real sense of humor becomes apparent when there is no space left; when you really have your back against the wall; when you think that it's all over now – if in this case you can still see to some degree a humorous side, then it is a real and true humor." The forecourt of the Jokhang, where dozens of Tibetans have positioned themselves to make their prostrations, is swathed with white mist of burnt juniper. Every day for four months they practice this exercise of humility designed to subdue ego-grasping and destroy delusion. On the kora around the Jokhang we see a young Tibetan woman with her small son. Connected to his mother's arm by a nylon string, the child follows her prostrations. Around the Jokhang, Buddhism is alive in all generations.

Full of sorrow I stand in the ruins of the Shol district below the Potala. Intentionally, the Chinese occupying forces leave the valuable architecture of this historical part of town to dilapidation. I remember the Dalai Lama's words: "For once it is my firm conviction that the power of the rifle barrels is only temporary. But the power of truth increases more and more with time." Until 1997, this district was completely intact and inhabited. Now it is an example of the power and ignorance of

Chinese dictatorship. Matthieu Ricard describes the situation accurately:

No more activity on the outside because there is no more activity on the inside.

Tourists do not even notice, because the gates of Shol district are closed and the main entrance to the Potala shifted to the rear side. The attitude of Lhasa's inhabitants has changed. The

forced resettlement of about 10 million Han Chinese in Tibet has meanwhile left its distinct marks. The Tibetan people have become a minority in their own country; Tibet's capital resembles a Chinese supermarket.

With horror, the Tibetans witnessed the opening of the new railroad line Beijing – Lhasa. The ambitious project, which was completed in 2006, will be the deathblow to the Tibetan culture.

LHASA 117

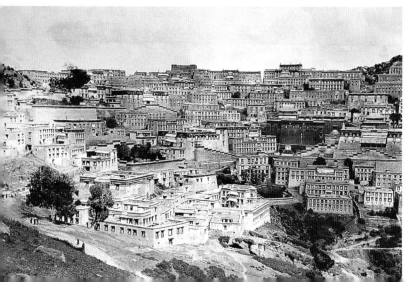

The last sunrays of the day seeped and pushed their way through the thunderclouds and bathed Ganden Monastery in a warm evening light. Ganden means 'Joyful', thus called by the same name as the spheres where the Buddhas dwell before they return to the world for the last time to teach people the Dharma. Ganden, 65 kilometers (40 miles) away from Lhasa, is situated at an altitude of 4,375 meters (14,350 feet); it towers in a basin-shaped valley on the upper Kyichu river. The monastery was the religious center of the Gelugpa school. Founded by Tsongkhapa in 1409, it quickly developed and became an important university. Within ten years following the founding of Ganden, two other Gelugpa monasteries, each housing about 8,000 monks, were established in the Lhasa valley: Drepung in 1416, and Sera in 1419. Thus the Gelugpas, the Virtuous, gained a great deal of influence in Tibet.

I look over Ganden and remember Sonam Yospel. Here he spent twelve years of his life. Here he had to witness how Chinese soldiers razed the monastery; how they destroyed statues because they believed they would find hidden offering substances inside. After Sonam's escape, during the years of the 'Cultural Revolution,' Ganden was completely destroyed. Until 1978, there were only ruins left; it was strictly forbidden to enter these sites. On asking oneself why human beings are trying to eradicate cultures in such ideological madness, an answer could be found in what the great Tibetan master Dilgo Khyentse Rinpoche said, who himself had to escape from Tibet:

A beautiful country is a dreamlike illusion; it is futile to grasp at it.
As long as the inner forces of negative emotions have not been defeated, fighting off the outer enemies will never end!

About 50 of the former 200 buildings of the monastery have been reconstructed and are now a home to 270 monks. They are only allowed to follow their studies when under strict supervision by the Chinese. I leave them in their unawareness about the cause of my visit, because I do not want to put anybody in danger. Three days later my journey to Mount Kailash begins.

Lhasa – Changes of a City
By Klemens Ludwig

North of the Potala Palace visitors to Lhasa are witness to scenes resembling a historical movie. Men and women with prayer wheels in long and well-worn leather coats are on a pilgrimage along the blacktop road. Although the road is wide, there is not much space for these pilgrims, who move along by means of full-length prostrations. Cars and bicycles dominate the picture; the house-fronts in the background proclaim the world of globalization: Toyota, Mitsubishi and VW brand names shine their neon-lights; China's economic power is what comes to mind. Two over-dimensional golden yaks are reminiscent of Tibet, a monument of high symbolic value: in Lhasa all that is Tibetan is rendered museum-like in appearance.

Nevertheless, the pilgrims resembling relics from a long ago past follow their path. Since time immemorial, the Lingkhor, a major pilgrimage route, leads along this way, and it is not only the old people who follow it. Destination of the pilgrims is the Jokhang Temple in Lhasa's center. From early morning to late at night people circumambulate the temple district according to the old tradition, alongside long rows of stalls where devotional objects and religious pictures are offered for sale. Even here, space has become constricted. There has been heavy building activity all over the town center for years. All Tibetan houses are demolished and replaced by functional concrete buildings. However: "Except for the Chinese immigrants the government does not build any houses. Entire streets have fallen victim to the bulldozers. Now there are multi-story shopping malls and residential blocks which we cannot afford to rent," complains someone who wants to keep his name a secret for obvious reasons.

Since the beginning of the last decade of the 20th century, Beijing has invested several hundred million dollars, year by year, to rob the town of its historical and cultural identity. More than 400 of 600 historical buildings have been torn down since the invasion. Among them is the Tromsikhang Palace, which had been constructed by the 6th Dalai Lama north of the Jokhang in the early 18th century. Although the fabric of the palace was still very good and it had even been classified as highly worthy of protection by the UNESCO, it nonetheless fell victim to the bulldozers. According to a study of

the "Center on Housing Rights and Evictions," which is supported by the United Nations, Tibetan settlements have shrunk to merely two percent of Lhasa's area, which meanwhile has extended to 53 square kilometers (20 square miles).

At the beginning of the last decade of the 20th century, the UNESCO suggested to classify several buildings in Lhasa as World Heritage, which means a certain public protection from further destruction. Among others, the Potala Palace and the Jokhang Temple were added to the list. The government agreed to the Potala Palace only, because around the Jokhang Temple they did not want to accept any restrictions. The nomination of the Potala Palace just came right for them to demonstrate how engaged they are in the conservation of Tibetan culture. In December 1994, the Potala was officially declared UNESCO World Heritage and subsequently underwent fundamental renovation. For the reopening ceremony, besides high functionaries from Beijing, also representatives of the tourism industry from Hong Kong came traveling. The event was cleverly designed to fit their needs: karaoke competitions, souvenir stalls, gambling and horse racing were entertaining the masses, and in no way was it reminiscent of the Palace's original purpose.

Nevertheless, the surroundings of the Potala Palace were not saved from destructive action. Until the end of the eighties, there existed the Shol district at its south face, which had been laid out three hundred years before to protect the Palace from intruders. Due to its favorable location however, Shol became a very popular place for business. In 1990, its 1,000 inhabitants had to make room for an amusement park, a red-light district with bars, karaoke events, discothèques and adjoining brothels. Since Deng Xiaoping's time, the opportunity to make money, in every sector whatsoever, has become one of the greatest freedoms in the Chinese sphere of influence.

Left: Chinese tourists taking photographs of each other in Tibetan costumes with the Potala in the background.
Right: The systematic renovation of the old regions gives Lhasa a Chinese face.

> We should learn to consider the world as our home.
> When we realize that we are one, the world will be our home.
> We have to feel responsibility for every part of the world.
> This is the only way to ease the sufferings that we encounter
> these days.
>
> THICH NHAT HANH

TOWARD MOUNT KAILASH

June 22, 2004, Banakshol Hotel, Lhasa

Eight o'clock in the morning – my baggage and camera equipment are stowed away in the Toyota four-wheel drive. Rinzen-la starts the engine; for many years he has been my driver. "Kang Rinpoche," he says, beaming. "Ngatsho Kang Rinpoche la drogi yö," I reply: "Yes, we are going to Mount Kailash!" Slowly the land cruiser moves through the streets of Lhasa, which fill with life at the first rays of sun. We pass a huge new Chinese department store, and observe the staff assembling in rank and then filing at the main entrance, like a military unit awaiting the morning roll-call inspection. Half shouting, half singing, the excited manager tries to introduce his crew to the art of self-motivation, followed by a joint two-kilometer (1.25-miles) run through the streets of Lhasa – in full sales associate uniform.

Our destination for today is Samye, Tibet's first and oldest monastery at the banks of the Yarlung Tsangpo. Carrying a lot of sand, the river has formed a one-kilometer wide riverbed. Suddenly we see a yak-hide boat on the water. We stop and wait at the riverside. The ferryman carries it ashore on his back and lays it down to dry. "It seems to be my vocation to ferry people over the river," he says in a silent voice that sounds content.

This is what the 14th Dalai Lama would say: "Peace in the world comes from peace in the individual. If you are at ease in a natural way and in peace with yourself, then you will be frank and open toward your fellow beings. And this is exactly the foundation of world peace."

We cross over the Tsangpo, and from afar we can see the golden pagoda roof of Samye Monastery. At the time of its construction at the end of the 8th century, natural disasters occurred repeatedly, walls collapsed, floods and earthquakes suggested that earth and water spirits were obstructing the building activities. Therefore, the great guru and magician Padmasambhava from India was called upon for help. Powerfully and skillfully he subdued all the spirits and demons.

Moreover, he even committed them to serve the Buddhist purpose.

The powers that move the universe are not different from those that move the human mind.

Anagarika Govinda's contemplations on Samye are clear and to the point. The monastery was built in the form of a huge mandala; the main temple in the middle represents Mount Meru, the center of the universe; four chortens symbolize the four continents of Tibetan cosmology. Samye's perimeter, the "iron wall," secludes the inner sacred sphere of nirvana from samsara, the outer sphere of the eternal cycle of living, dying and rebirth.

June 26, 2004, Gyantse, Tibet

It is the 17th Karmapa's birthday today. Hundreds of Tibetan pilgrims come to visit the Kumbum Chorten in Gyantse, the great three-dimensional mandala.

Little Purbu looks at his butter lamp and clasps it with his tiny hands. "Om mani padme hum, om mani padme hum," again and again he recites the mantra of the Buddha of compassion. Following his mother, he enters the stairs of the chorten. Two colorfully painted Dharma protectors make his blood run cold. He puts his butter lamp down and prostrates himself three times.

Merely four years of age, his body language mirrors some kind of understanding. How does the searching for reincarnations feel for a Lama? Very often the memory of former lives will have spoken to them through the children they had before them. Smiling to myself, I observed little Purbu's thirst for action and become absorbed in Jack Kornfield's thought:

Our children are our meditation.

June 28, 2004, Shigatse, Tibet

Morning mist over Shigatse causes the smoke of countless chimneys to rise up very slowly. Regardless of the spectacular misty morning show, the pagoda roofs of Tashilhunpo Monastery glimmer in the first sunrays. It is not only the architecture of the monastery complex, that gives rise to a unique harmonious atmosphere, but also the innumerable rock paintings at the roadside lend a hand.

In Tashilhunpo the Panchen Lama resided, the second highest Lama of Tibet. Gendun Drup, Tsongkhapa's nephew, founded the Gelugpa monastery in 1447. More than 4,000 monks used to study there, but today only 300 yellow-hats live within the monastery walls.

Chinese supervision, however, is omnipresent. One has to remember that the 11th Panchen Lama is considered the youngest political prisoner in the world. In 1995, the Dalai Lama officially acknowledged Chokyi Nyima, who was only six years of age at this time, as the reincarnation of the late 10th Panchen Lama. Nevertheless, the Chinese government enthroned a candidate of their own and deported Chokyi Nyima to a place still unknown today.

July 4, 2004

We left Shigatse four days ago. Since Lhatse, asphalt roads are long behind us, now the surfaces alternate between sand and stone. Again and again we encounter mostly overloaded trucks full of Tibetan pilgrims. Crammed on mattresses, tent canvases and provisions, exposed to sun, wind and sand for weeks without any protection, but remarkably still at ease, they look forward to their arrival at Manasarovar Lake.

Lunch time! In the middle of nowhere, we stop at a small stone hut. I enter the "restaurant" and immediately find myself in a seemingly unreal setting.

I come to sit opposite the father and son of the house. Not only are they identically clothed at the occasion, but their hair-

rainbow and the face of the Buddha of compassion, Avalokiteshvara, who is in the same line of incarnations with the Dalai Lama. Thus, indirectly the Dalai Lama is pictured on the wall, although this is strictly prohibited by the Chinese government. A clever solution and definitely the Chinese will never notice. Exactly as the Buddha says:

We are what we think! Whatever we are originates from our thoughts.

For there is a Tibetan saying that goes like this: "How do you keep a sheep under control? – You give it a large grazing field!" I contemplate the situation: two Tibetan generations, old and

styles, necklaces and white bracelets are also exactly the same. The funniest detail surrounding the situation is the presence of the two posters behind them. In one, Mao Zedong looks out and in the other, there is the Potala Palace crowned with a

young, father and son, past and present. They let their hearts speak – whoever has eyes can see.

"Skillful means," I think, "the ancient principle of Tibetan Buddhism."

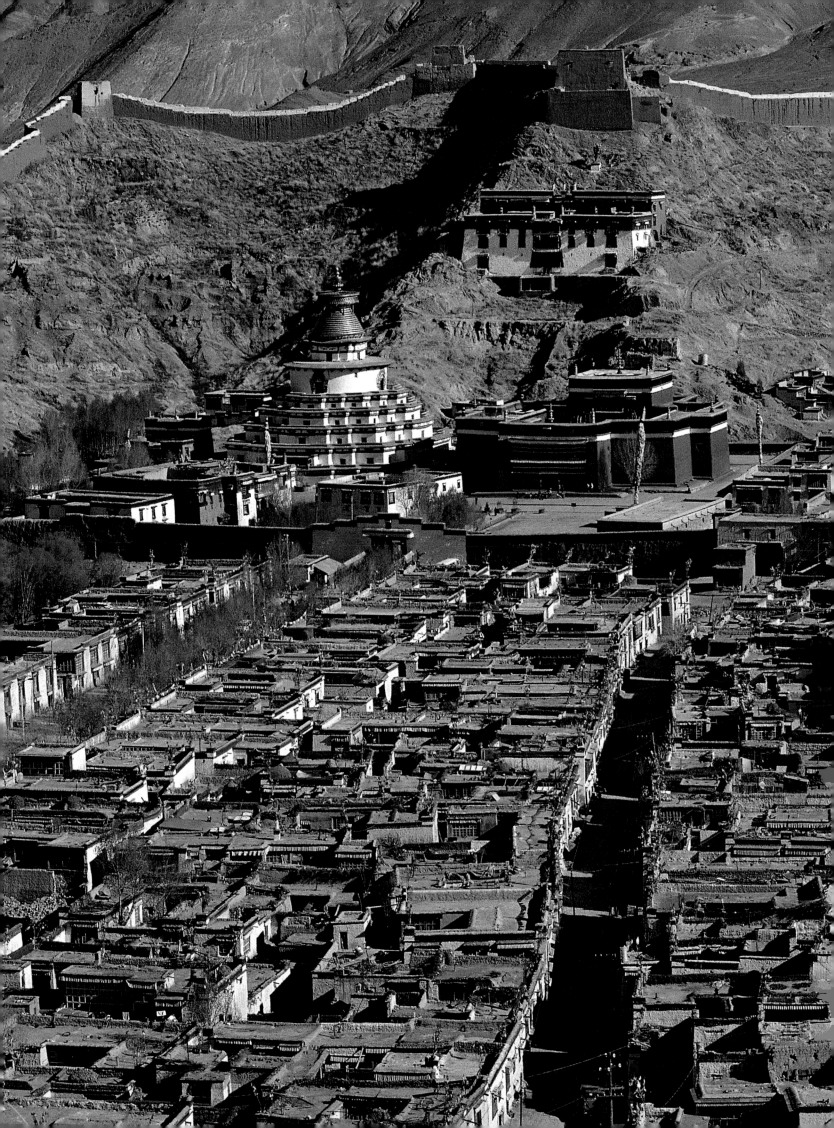

Gyantse's Kumbum Chorten

By Klemens Ludwig

Before the Chinese invasion, Gyantse was somewhat different compared to its two larger sister towns Lhasa and Shigatse, which were dominated by monasteries and monks. Gyantse, a major exit on the way to Nepal, Sikkim and India, became important commercially. At the time of British colonization, the Southern neighbor India was Tibet's most important trading partner. Thus, since long, an atmosphere of free thought has characterized Gyantse; and when in the twenties of the last century the young and innovative tried to break the monasteries' educational monopoly and establish a secular school, Gyantse offered the most favorable situation. In Lhasa as well as in Shigatse such a provocation of tradition would have been impossible. In Gyantse, nevertheless, the experiment lasted for four years, then even there the school had to close down under the pressure of the religious state and with the assistance of a natural event!

During a soccer game, in itself unacceptable for the custodians of tradition, a heavy hailstorm loomed up, notably unusual for the season. The players were hit by hailstones the size of table-tennis balls. Excitedly, the monks were able to convince the public that this was caused by the gods showing their anger toward such mundane activity. Thus, the first educational reform in Tibet ended; still Gyantse remained more open for worldly interests than the two "sacred" cities.

Moreover, most of the foreigners who were staying in Tibet in the first half of the 20th century – mostly British – lived in Gyantse.

Additionally, in Gyantse there is also an impressive monastery complex, the construction of which began in the 14th century. In the times of Tibetan independence, this institution also mirrored the spirit of the city, because it was a home for 18 monasteries of the different Buddhist schools, which coexisted in perfect harmony. None of these was nearly as big as the important monasteries in Lhasa or Shigatse, but together they were a good example of what one could call practical religious tolerance. In the 18th century at the peak of monastic life in Gyantse, about 3,000 monks lived on the compound; but after the Chinese invasion only about 800 remained. The most impressive building is the 15th century Kumbum chorten.

The 35 meters (115 feet) high 14-floor construction is among the few monastic buildings of the country which can be admired in its original form, because it has not fallen victim to the vast destructions after the 1959-uprising. The Kumbum chorten, also named 'Stupa of the 100,000 Buddhas,' does not have the form of a temple but resembles an inordinately large reliquary. At first, Buddha's eyes looking in all directions cast a spell on the visitors. They are painted on the outer walls of the seventh story and can even look slightly threatening at times – depending on one's own mood.

The fact that Kumbum chorten can – and should actually be entered, is another reason for its uniqueness: on the way to the very top, the wisdom of Tibetan Buddhism is revealed in its completeness. There are 108 doors, the holy number of Buddhism, which is also traceable in many units of measurement. The lower floors comprise of 68 chapels. There are countless wall paintings, statues and ornaments, each a piece of art in its own right, depicting scenes of the Buddhist world in all its facets. This was the way the life story of the Buddha, the spreading of the teachings in Tibet, the magical displays of the great masters Padmasambhava or Atisha, or tantric ritual were made accessible to the visitors, who in former times were illiterate. Consistently the symbolism is so rich that even experts cannot fully grasp it. A great deal of space is devoted to the pictures that display the path to enlightenment. Even more so, the complete stupa with all its mystical references seems like the path to enlightenment itself. Winding from floor to floor the path leads upward past further and further pieces of art. Eventually, atop there is a shining jewel and flame, the symbol of enlightenment.

Left: View of Gyantse's old region and the monastery complex of Palkhor Chode.
Right: The 35-meter (115 feet) high Kumbum Chorten; 68 shrine rooms and chapels give an impression of the complete Indian and Tibetan pantheon.

We can experience it all over again:
The present moment is a wonderful moment.
Fewer fixations of volition and intellect,
letting go, renouncing greed,
? all this increases our being, each moment.

THICH NHAT HANH

LAKE MANASAROVAR

July 6, 2004, Lake Manasarovar, West Tibet

"Tso Rinpoche," Sonam Tsering laughs. "The Precious Lake!" Sonam's mother ladles the holy water from Lake Manasarovar by the spoonful. Later, when they will return from their pilgrimage to their home village in Amdo, they want to use the precious liquid for religious rituals. Most probably each villager will take a good drop from the container immediately on their arrival.

"The water has miraculous healing power, like the fish from the lake," Sonam explains to me. "Today I have found two dry fish. They are washed up along the shore in stormy weather. We Tibetans look for such fish at the lakeshore. In the form of powder, they are precious medicine. Today is my lucky day!"

In Tibet "Sernya" – the sign of two goldfish facing each other – is one of the Eight Auspicious Symbols. Fish, except when offered by the 'Lu,' the highest gods of the rivers and lakes, are considered inviolable by the Tibetans. Since the time of the invasion, Chinese soldiers fishing at Lake Manasarovar are an everyday occurrence. Whereas Herbert Tichy's and Anagarika Govinda's travel books have accounted for animals in abundance in the Kailash region, it is a sad fact today that nearly all of them were eradicated by the Chinese invaders.

Sonam and her family had set out from their home country Amdo eight months before. They went 2,000 kilometers (1,240 miles) on foot to reach the shores of Lake Manasarovar.

As female and male counterparts, Manasarovar and Kailash are inseparably connected. Situated at an altitude of 4,558 meters (14,950 feet) and as such the world's highest sweet-water lake, Manasarovar with its turquoise waters is looked upon as being a mirror of contemplation by Buddhists and Hindus alike.

It takes pilgrims three or four days to circumambulate the lake by way of the 88-kilometers-long (55 miles) sacred kora. At one time, eight monasteries stood and were the ornaments of the shores. However, sadly even here in Tibet's far west, the Cultural Revolution's frenzy of destruction did not come to a halt. All eight monasteries on Lake Manasarovar were razed to the ground.

Majestically Gosul Monastery towers on the steep rocks of the South Western shore. It is one of five, which have been reconstructed. I enjoy the fantastic view of the lake and watch the crystal-clear waters, the passing pilgrims, the cackling wild geese. Today, it is His Holiness' birthday; I read in one of his books:

There is nothing that is permanent. The sun and the moon rise and fall; the bright day is followed by the dark night. Everything changes from hour to hour.

Slowly the sun sinks on the horizon, making the Himalaya's magical intensity of colors visible. The pebbles washed on the shore by the waters resemble an open treasure box filled with turquoise, sapphire, emerald, lapis lazuli, corals and amber. I try to catch up with Sonam's group of pilgrims. Three days later at dusk, I reach their camp whilst pitch-black threatening clouds are hanging above.

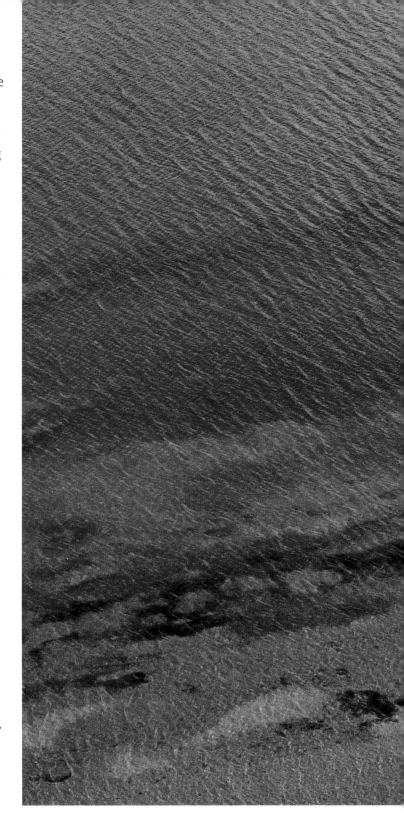

From the beginning of the kora, I have chosen to spend the night out in the open air underneath the stars and the sky with views over the holy lake and Mount Kailash. Here I find time and space to reflect upon the bygone days. I keep looking across to Mount Kailash with the one question in mind: Will I be able to solve the Golden Tara's secret? Sogyal Rinpoche's words deeply move my mind: You can find peace only when you are free from hope.

With views of the dramatic monsoon sky, smiling to myself, I note Kalu Rinpoche's words in my daybook:

The mind in its ordinary state can be compared with a sky that is obscured by layers of clouds concealing its true nature.

For 18 months, I have followed the traces of the Golden Tara. The journey takes away my hopes and puts modesty in its place. Whatever I will find, it is already existent within me.

At noon on the fourth day, we reach the "Bird Monastery," Tschui Gompa, on the North Western shore of the lake. The small monastery was built on a hill where Padmasambhava is said to have spent the last seven days of his life. The old walls silently keep watch over Buddhist scriptures of bygone times.

Milarepa

Mount Kailash
(Gang Rinpoche)
6638 m

Shiva

Dölma La
5660 m

Tichung

Dira Phug
Gönpa

Silwatsel

Kadrome truki dzingbu

Gonpo Pang

Serdung Chuksum La
5859 m

Khadroe-Sanglam La

13 Golden Stupas

Lham Chu

Dütsi menqyi
tso Kapala

Chöku Gönpa

Zuthrul Phug Gönpa

Topchen

Serlung Gönpa

Gyangdrag Gönpa

Chöten Kangni

Darpoche

Dzong Chu

Sershong

Chagtselgang

Drangser Drangmar

Lha Chu

DARCHEN

Tibetan Medical &
Astro Institute

4670 m

B A R K H A   T H A N K A

Barkha (Barga)

Langbona Gönpa

Horch

Ganga Chu

Cherkip Gönpa (Ruine)

Chiu Gönpa

Manasarovar Lake

Rakas Tal

4582 m

Seralung Gönpa

Gossul Gönpa

4572 m

Tag Tsangpo

Trugo Gönpa

Gurla La

Gurla Chu

Gurla Mandhata
7694 m

A. Rohweder

Kailash and Manasarovar
By Franz Binder

None of the countless holy mountains of this world can measure up to the standard of Mount Kailash in the far West of Tibet. Although its 6,714 meters (22,022 feet) seem almost miniature compared to the Central Himalaya's peaks, it is spiritually many times more important. To four religions of Asia it represents the hub of the world, the throne of the Gods, the center of the mystical continent Jambudvipa, the manifestation of Mount Meru: to Hindus, Buddhists, Jains – an Indian religion of ascetics ?, and Bonpos – Tibet's original religion. Like an archetype, Kailash is deeply embodied in Asia's consciousness. It was probably a holy site of forgotten cultures, even before its name came shining up from the darkness of time, even before the oral tradition found its expression in the Hindu epics Ramayana and Mahabharata: "There is no mountain range like Himaltschal, for within it there are Kailasa and Manasarovar."

Not only Mount Kailash enjoys such veneration. Kang Rinpoche, the "Snow Jewel," as the Tibetans call the foremost of all mountains, is part of a natural mandala which spreads below its Southern slopes, enchanting with breathtaking beauty. Whereas Mount Kailash is considered the throne of male deities, the Gurla Mandhata facing it is the seat of the goddess Lhamo Yangchen. Barkha, the high plateau in between, adds two lakes to this natural mandala – Manasarovar and Rakshastal, manifestations of the elemental dualistic principle: Lake Manasarovar stands for the power of light and consciousness; for Brahma himself, as the legend goes, has created it from his mind. In the West of the "King of all Sacred Lakes," Rakshastal, the manifestation of lunar energies, of the night, of the unconscious and of evil demons, shines darkly. Ganga Chu, a natural channel, connects the two lakes. When it is water-bearing, Tibetans consider this a very auspicious sign for the snow land's future, a sign that the male Manasarovar and the female Rakshastal are associated like bride and groom.

A further geographical feature characterizes the Kailash mandala: four rivers have their sources near the holy mountain – Sutlej, Karnali, Indus and Tsangpo (Brahmaputra). This, however, points out the function of Mount Kailash as an earthly portrayal of the cosmic Mount Meru, the axis of the world, which penetrates all levels of existence from the depths of hell to the heavenly realms of the gods. All four religions considering Kang Rinpoche a holy mountain have attached great detail to the myth of the center of the universe, which is at home in many cultures. For the pilgrims who circumambulate Mount Kailash in veneration, it is also the seat of powerful deities. For Hindus it is the throne of Shiva, who, absorbed in deep meditation, resides there as the master of yogis, the destroyer of ignorance, as the one who dissolves the profane, together with his Shakti, the goddess Parvati, and surrounded by a magnificent circular city of gods. Furthermore the tantric deity Chakrasamvara, venerated as the master of Kailash by the pilgrims, resides there in union with his consort Vajravarahi. The portrayal of these deities in union with their female equivalents is a visual metaphor for the inseparability of the cosmic primal elements of male and female, two in one. For the Jains, however, Mount Kailash is the place where the first of their 24 Tirthamkaras, the "forerunner," has attained enlightenment. Eventually, for the Bonpos the "Kang Tise" is a nine-floor Svastika pyramid, the soul of the snow land.

Even if many pilgrims are hardly able to comprehend the philosophical and cosmological concepts connected to Mount Kailash, simple farmers and nomads still enjoy their share of the transcendent energy concentrating at the mountain, and experience the spiritual purification and transformation of the kora, the 53-kilometer-long (33 miles) circumambulation representing a complete cycle of life, death and rebirth.

Left: Panoramic map of Mount Kailash by Arne Rohweder, www.geckomaps.com
Right: Mount Kailash towering the Transhimalaya Range; view of Lake Manasarovar; the Kailash north face with its protecting mountains Avalokiteshvara and Vajrapani near Dirapuk Gompa; the evening sun shining on the holy mountain.

Learn how to hold the present moment! Don't steal away, don't escape into the delusion of the past or the future.

Concentrate your mind where you are, with a keen consciousness on the very moment.

This is where we are. There is no other place than right here.

DRUKPA RINPOCHE

MOUNT KAILASH

July 11, 2004, Dirapuk Gompa, Mount Kailash

"Kang Rinpoche kora dun – I have done the kora around Kailash seven times." Young Dorje seems happy and content. "This morning we have set off for round number eight, probably the last one," says his mother. She puts her arm on his shoulders. "So, today we are traveling the Eightfold Noble Path," she pinches Dorje's neck. The Eightfold Noble Path is the core teaching of Buddhist ethics, Buddha's instruction for liberation. Presumably there is no other place to be found for contemplating liberation more suitable than Mount Kailash, the center of the universe. I recall the eight rules in my mind: right outlook, right intention, right speech, right action, right livelihood, right pursuit, right mindfulness, right concentration. Like a pyramid of snow in the background of mother and son,

the 6,714-meter-high (22,022 feet) Kailash rises up into the universe. It is the center of Tibetan cosmology, the earth's axis, the greatest natural mandala of all time. Since immeasurable time, Mount Kailash has had enormous mythical power on the people of India and Tibet. It is one of the most important pilgrimage destinations for Tibetan Buddhists, for Hindus, Jains and Bonpos – seat of the Buddhas and Bodhisattvas. The sun and the moon are in orbit around it. It is the mandala of bliss. On its peak, according to the Tibetans, Heruka, the wrathful manifestation of Buddha wisdom, is seated on his throne. For Hindus it is the throne of Shiva, the God of destruction and restoration. For me Mount Kailash is a moment of insight: without beginning or end.

On the 15th day of the fourth month, according to the Tibetan calendar, Tibetans celebrate Buddha's enlightenment: Saga

sounds simple and comprehensible; but very often exactly this is what makes it the most difficult learning. All over again, our

We have the present moment only, this unique and everlasting moment, which opens up and develops before our eyes, day and night.

Dawa Festival. On that day, the water pole is erected at Mount Kailash. For thousands of pilgrims this means a moment of joy and humility. The advice of the Buddhist monk Jack Kornfield

deluded thinking indulges in the phantom world of the past, senselessly getting entangled in future plans. This way we cut ourselves off from the sacred present moment.

A high level of concentration is needed to erect the huge water pole. Hundreds of helpers slowly pull it into an upright position. "Lha gyalo – Victory to the Gods!" Papers printed with prayers fill the air. The master of ceremonies takes special care that the pole, the symbol of good luck and peace, is fixed in a precise vertical position. In spite of the omnipresent Chinese military, the pilgrims calmly circumambulate the water pole, centered in the present moment.

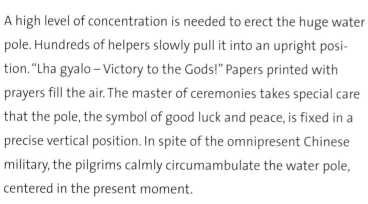

"Milarepa ki do," Sonam's Uncle points at a wayside stone. "Milarepa's footprint," he murmurs and sits horseback in the hollow. The Tibetan Yogi and magician Milarepa has, like Padmasambhava, remained in meditation on Mount Kailash for a long time and has left his traces. The pilgrim passes dozens of such sacred stones on his kora around the mountain. No Tibetan ever doubts the mystical and magical powers of these stones, for they are tools and benchmarks on their way to realization.

"Who performs the circumambulation of Mount Kailash with absolute devotion and concentration experiences a complete cycle of life and rebirth," I read in Anagarika Govinda's book "The Way of the White Clouds."

The Tibetan master Kalu Rinpoche describes it this way:

Farewell and death are just different names for new beginning and life. Whatever you have left behind, you will find in another form all over again.

Since Lake Manasarovar, I accompany Sonam's family on their pilgrimage. Together, we have done the kora around Mount Kailash for three times already.

"Normal" pilgrims take two to three days to complete the 53-kilometer-long (33 miles) circumambulation; tough Tibetans even do it in one day.

Sonam's pilgrimage group travels with only light baggage. A few blankets and pots, the inevitable goat-leather bellows for fire making, some roasted barley flour and dried yak meat, a bar of pressed tea, butter and salt. The remainder, the pilgrim carries on his body; mostly layers of two pairs of pants and three sweaters; better too warm than too cold. Temperatures below freezing at night and frozen water places he accepts with a strong sense of humor. Deeply at ease, for him time and space are as wide as the sky.

I feel deep contentment and read in Jack Kornfield's book: "Desire what you have and not what you don't have. Then you will experience true wealth."

We pack up and set off – everything fits together; whether old or young, the strong sense of ease is striking.

In the Lha Chu valley, we come across nuns who perform the kora by means of full prostrations. It takes them three weeks, Ganesh, the Elephant God, will be the witness.

We spend the night below Dirapuk Gompa. The following morning, we set off early and reach the 5,100-meter-high (16,728 feet) charnel ground of Shiwa Tsal before noon. Tibetans lie on the icy ground for one hour; in meditation they go through the 49 days of the bardos, the intermediate states after death in which one meets with Yama, the Lord of Judgment and Death. With his weighing scales he evaluates the negative and positive actions of the past life. The deceased sees one of the six realms of existence in his mirror and has to be reborn there. This is what the Buddha said on the subject:

You are what you have done; and you will be, what you do now.

Padmasambhava goes even further: "If you want to know your past life, look at your present situation; if you want to know your future life, look at your present action."

Here at Shiwa Tsal, the Tibetans leave behind pieces of clothing and personal items of any kind. Some pilgrims even cut off some of their hair or offer a few drops of blood. This signifies a purification of negative action and is a sign of humility. However, to be reborn one has to die first: this is what the pilgrims symbolically do here at Shiwa Tsal.

One hour later, we reach the rock formations of Bardo Grang. Cheerfully the Tibetans creep and squeeze themselves through the narrow gaps of trial. To be stuck is a sign of too many negative past actions.

The path rapidly winds up to the 5,636-meter-high (18,486 feet) Dolma-la, the pass of the Goddess Tara. For the pilgrims this is the point of decision between life and death. We reach Tara's rock on the pass at noon. Sonam's sister puts her hands together and recites Tara's mantra: "Om tare tuttare ture svaha." All look happy and content. A new cycle begins.

During the last seven years, I have been here at Mount Kailash four times, and today I climb the high pass of Dolma-la for the 13th time. Now the road is open for me to do the inner kora, because only after 13 circumambulations one is authorized to enter the innermost part of the mandala. Urgyen, the son of my old friend Tashi from Tschiu Gompa, will go with me.

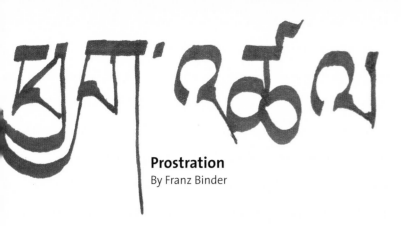

Prostration
By Franz Binder

Travelers to the Tibetan cultural area can watch a specific form of religious devotion in monasteries, temples and sacred places. There is no documentation about Tibet which does not include pictures of believers who fold their hands in a quick sequence above their heads, in front of their foreheads and chests, then go to their knees to touch the ground with their heads, or stretch out the body full length, remain in this position of humility for a short moment and then get up again and repeat the exercise over and over again.

At particularly sacred places like the Jokhang in Lhasa, there are always crowds of people to be seen who practice this exercise without interruption. Some of them even use prostrations as an effortful means of moving forward. With their bodies, they take measure of the circular walks around monasteries, temples and stupas, prostrating themselves, stretching out on the ground, rising again and starting the next prostration from the point where their fingertips have touched. Some believers, taking several weeks, cover even difficult pilgrimage paths in this way, like the 53-kilometer-long (33 miles) kora around the holy Mount Kailash. Especially tough pilgrims can travel even hundreds or thousands of kilometers like this to reach their destinations; they are on their way for years, regardless of cold, hunger, or difficult terrain. Repeatedly they stretch out on the ground with a scratching, scraping sound, whether it be a dirt road on the lonely high plains of the Changtang, a rocky path over a high pass, or the asphalt surface of an expressway in the middle of Lhasa. Yak-hide aprons and pieces of wood attached to hands and knees are designed to protect the body from injury.

Just how exhausting this can be was reported by August Gansser, who circumambulated Mount Kailash in 1936 in heavy rain and storm: "On our way we stumbled over a lama lying on the ground and nearly fell. In spite of his crawling exercise he had fallen asleep."

What serves as a picturesque object for the cameras of tourists and also as an easily accepted proof for the deep-rooted belief of simple Tibetans is, however, only the visible aspect of a religious exercise which is, by far, not restricted to popular belief. Whereas the outer gesture of prostrating equals the kow-tow, the Chinese form of venerating a dignitary or a deity, the spiritual meaning of this exercise goes much deeper. Although in the Tibetan cultural area, a high-ranking lama is also venerated by means of prostrating, such expression of honor is not so much for the person, but for his intellectuality, the spiritual principle which he embodies.

Prostrations have a far more important function within the practice of Ngondro, an exercise of four parts complementing each other, performed by monks and lay people for the purification of body, speech and mind in preparation for the tantric path. These are as follows: taking refuge and generating Bodhicitta, the mind of enlightenment; Vajrasattva practice to purify the aspect of speech; mandala offering to purify the mind and accumulate merit; Guru Yoga to focus on the path which is represented by the lama and his spiritual transmission lineage. Each of these exercises included in the Ngondro practice is performed at least one hundred thousand times.

Kyabdro, the first of the four parts, taking refuge in the Three Jewels – Buddha, Dharma (the teachings) and Sangha (the spiritual community), expresses itself physically by means of prostrations. The words of refuge are recited with every prostration. Moreover, the exercise is meant to overcome the characteristics of pride, to invoke in one's heart Bodhicitta, the aspiration toward enlightenment for the sake of all sentient beings, and to purify the adept from all karmic actions performed by the body. Prostration in connection with the taking of refuge is an elemental part of the Buddhist practice, and as such, it is not restricted to the beginning of the path; due to its deep meaning it is constantly renewed and performed all over again.

Left: The protective gear.
Right: Prostrations at Mount Kailash, on the icy pass of Dolma-la, and during the Saga Dawa Festival.

169

I am learning to see. I do not know why;
but matters are touching me deeper inside
and do not stop where they did before.
I have an inner space that I was not aware of.
Matters are penetrating now.
I do not know what is happening there.

RAINER MARIA RILKE

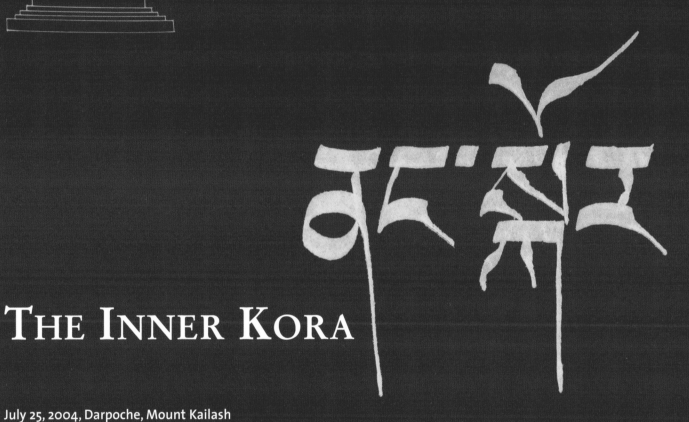

THE INNER KORA

July 25, 2004, Darpoche, Mount Kailash

We had an appointment in the Lhachu valley below Langchen Belphug, the Elephant Cave. In the early morning, there is a rustling noise at my bivouac tent and Urgyen looks expectantly inside. With his soft features, the long plaited hair, the huge Kampa knife and his Tibetan wraparound coat, he could be mistaken for a North American Navajo Indian. Urgyen has circumambulated Mount Kailash more than 50 times; he knows the outer kora well. Even so, he has never before ventured into the inner mandala. It seems that now the special occasion has finally come for him to approach Mount Kailash in this way. In the next two days, on Padmasambhava's birthday, we want to reach the 13 chortens at the South side.

We cross the Lhachu river at Darpoche and climb up toward the sky burial ground. Often I have sat here contemplating the cut up corpses and meditating on impermanence. "Even reflecting on death is considered morbid thinking in the West, as if it isn't dying that everybody on this earth is perfectly good at," Sogyal Rinpoche used to joke. Tibetans think that giving death serious thought creates space for a sense of humor. We cross the small pass leading to Seralung Monastery and see a mani stone in the valley below. A monk puts his head against the colored script and murmurs his mantra. The thumbs of his folded hands show inward, a gesture of overcoming the egoistic self.

July 26, Seralung Monastery

Urgyen and I spend the night on the pasture of Seralung Monastery at an altitude of 4,985 meters (16,351 feet). The gompa is like the entry gate to the inner kora. My thoughts revolve around the golden Tara. I remember Susan Taylor's words:

Thoughts are energy.
By means of your thinking you can create your own world or you can destroy it.

Outside our tents, there is a knee-deep carpet of blossoming edelweiss. At the same time, the rich meadows are a warning to beware of the approaching monsoon season and abrupt weather changes. We say farewell to the monks and continuously follow the course of the narrow Seralung Chu in the direction of Mount Kailash. There is a 1,000-meter-high (328 feet) climb to be mastered today.

The stony path winds up to the high valley. The steep slope of the riverbank obstructs our view of Mount Kailash. We keep our bearings by aiming at the Nandi promontory, Shiva's bull. Eventually, the river runs dry. We enter the realm of silence; for the first time ever, I can faintly imagine the meaning of the word emptiness.

I remember Longchenpa's words: "As everything is nothing more than appearance, perfect as it is, without characteristics like good or bad, to be accepted or rejected, one could burst

out laughing." I feel peaceful. My altimeter shows 5,500 meters (18,040 feet).

We have reached the Nandi South face; here the path splits off into the direction that is to take us around Nandi mountain. We go left and follow the inner kora clockwise.

The path spirals up rapidly, and we are faced with a cold wind which lures white clouds into its spell. Little figures of piled up stones direct us toward the mandala, fossil Bodhisattvas, forever mute and helpful.

"Kang Rinpoche," I hear Urgyen calling out far in front of me. A few minutes later, I catch up with my Tibetan friend; a wide valley stretches before our eyes. A shudder goes through me. I feel like I'm on another planet. Never have I experienced Mount Kailash as powerful as here. The throne of the Gods, the center of Tibetan cosmology, a place of absolute silence – powerful and awe-inspiring.

This is the moment when questions lose their importance and hopes become meaningless. In this very moment, I internalize Buddha Shakyamuni's words which I have read very often: "Sweet are the fruits of hope which is fulfilled. They who let go of hopes, however, live in peace. Desire creates suffering. Letting go of desire creates inner happiness." Two hours later we pitch our tents below the South face of Mount Kailash. Nightfall is quickly upon us. We can see the shape of the 13 chortens 100 meters (33 feet) above us. "Tomorrow is a holy day," Urgyen says to me, "it is Padmasambhava's birthday. He will guide and protect us." Solemnly we fall asleep. During the night, snow begins to fall; a thick white blanket covers the inner mandala.

I can feel pressure on my body; and I wake up. Something presses the tent to the ground. I push my hands up with all my might and perceive a heavy extensive weight over me. Then, a familiar feeling: we are snowed in! The protectors of the inner sphere are opposing us. What are we to expect at the 13 chortens? Is there still anything left I can hope for? When, if not now, can I put into practice what I have learnt during my odyssey? As Govinda quotes Novalis:

All that is visible is attached to the invisible, all that is audible is attached to the inaudible, all that is tangible is on the verge of the intangible; and maybe all one can think is attached to the unthinkable.

We pack and set off. Suddenly we hear a low rushing sound in the air. Looking up with a jerk, our blood runs cold. An avalanche comes thundering down in free fall from the 600-

next avalanche comes roaring down behind us. We are still some meters away from the place of the 13 chortens, where we will be safe. Then finally, we arrive! We collapse on the stony narrow ledge with exhaustion.

My gaze is lost in the vanishing line of the 13 chortens, which are protected by overhanging rocks. Urgyen touches each of the stupas with his forehead, folding his hands in deep prayer. Mani stones, kataks and butter lamps are placed in the corners and in the recesses of the rocky ledge; paper money is stuck to the walls. Then we discover it: a golden Tara – surrounded by tsatsas, offerings made from clay. I fall to my knees and hear

meter-high (1,968 feet) South face vertically above, and lands very close to us with a deafening roar. Urgyen continues through the deep snow, looking for a path in the steep wall rising up before him. Again the sound of thunder in the air; the

the Dalai Lama's words: "Who believes does not need any proof. Who does not believe is not satisfied with any proof." I can also feel the presence of Sonam Yospel: "Happiness is not a place to stay but a path to go!"

May all beings experience happiness and the causes of happiness;
May they all be free from suffering and the causes of suffering;
May they all never be separated from supreme happiness free of suffering;
May they all live in equanimity, without too much attachment and too much aversion;
And may they live in the knowledge of the sameness of all that lives.

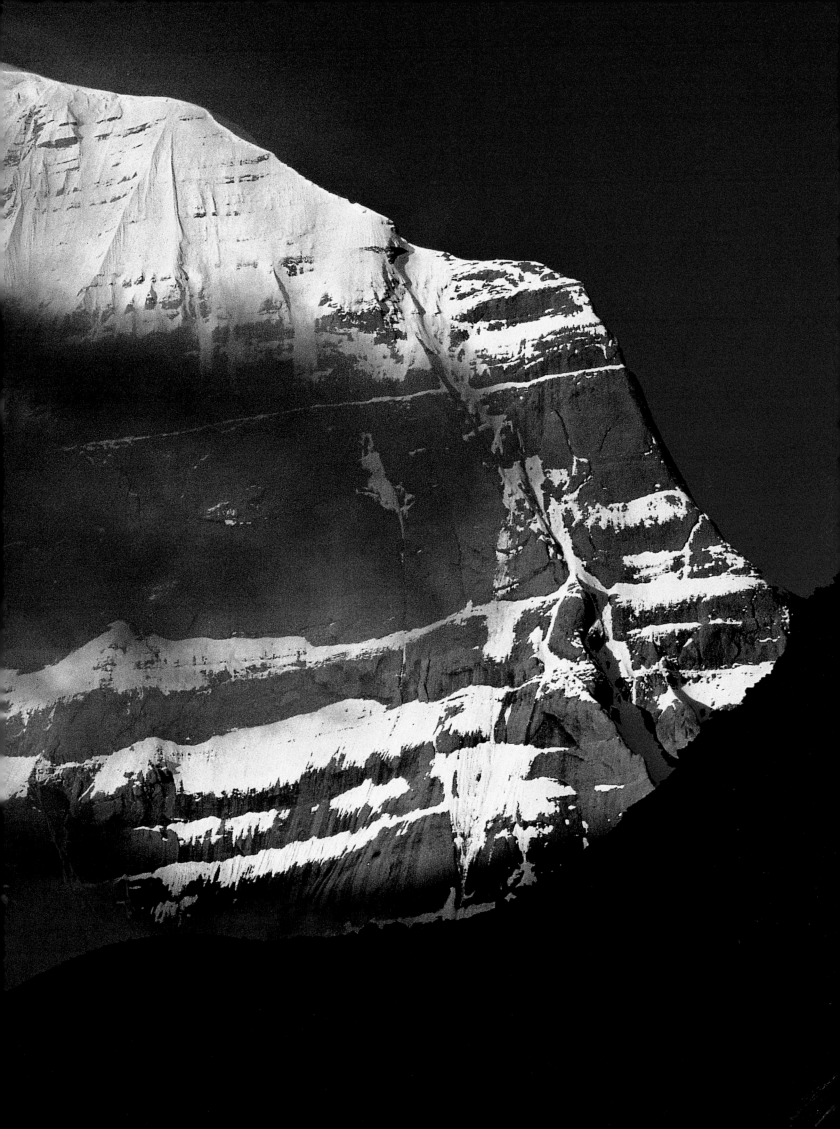

Three sadhus coming back from their pilgrimage to Muktinath. Near Tatopani they are crossing the long suspension bridge over the Kali Gandaki river. In the background the 6,987-meter-high (22,917 feet) Nilgiri mountain looms. Muktinath is one of the most sacred pilgrimage destinations in Nepal for Hindus and Buddhists alike. There, at an altitude of 3,985 meters (13,071 feet), all the five elements can be found in one place at a water spring.

2 | 3

At dawn, the monk Tsewang Jorges meditates at the old monastery of Shey in the Leh valley. In Ladakh, also called West Tibet or Little Tibet, one encounters Tibetan Buddhist architecture in its original beauty.

18 | 19

Near Hubli in South India, the two large Gelugpa monasteries Drepung and Ganden are situated. The wide sky extends over a tropically hot jungle. As the sun goes down, hundreds of monks recite the Buddhist scriptures and memorize them for their next exams.

8 | 9

The restricted area of 'Upper Mustang' is situated in the upper Kali Gandaki valley. Here, one can observe the Mustang Chorten, with its roof a shelter from sun and snow. The old capital Lo Mantang is still governed by a Raja, though he is under the King of Nepal.

20 | 21

Tashi and Karma, the two little novices, entered Lingshed Monastery when they were six years old. Young monks can experience a childhood of absolute happiness in the monasteries; there happens a lot of fun and laughter. Nevertheless, there are also duties, but they are quite different from the busy everyday school life of children in the West.

10 | 11

Dolka Tsering was on pilgrimage for over six months. Making a once-in-a-lifetime journey on foot, she went from Amdo to West Tibet to circumambulate Lake Manasarovar and Mount Kailash. During the kora, her Mani Chokhor, the prayer cylinder, rarely rested.

22 | 23

A sand mandala is a cosmogram and a psychogram, a path of self-realization for the monks who create it. At the same time, it is a symbol for the single cosmic law that nothing is permanent, that everything constantly changes. To make a mandala takes about one week, and after a puja it is swept together and the sand is poured into the river.

12 | 13

Summer impressions from Ladakh: in Ladakh and Zanskar a child's yellow cap indicates that it is a baby girl wearing it. Her mother has lovingly attached kauri shells to the cap; the little girl's soul can hide inside when bothered by demons. The needles protect her from the 'grip' of evil spirits.

36 | 37

In Ladakh and Zanskar there is no lack of joy and laughter, even when working on the fields. The deep-green barley fields in the fertile parts are in contrast to the colors of the desert highlands. Roasted barley called tsampa is the staple food in the entire Tibetan cultural area.

38 | 39

On a full moon night in August, hundreds of shamans meet at the sacred mountain lakes of Gosainkund in the Langtang area of the Northern Himalayas in Nepal. With their magical drums and bells they invoke spirits and heal people from sicknesses. The tradition of the shamans is passed on from father to son, sometimes to the daughter, as well.

74 | 75

The young girl Tugme Angmo of the Zanskari village Pidmo baking Chapatis from roasted barley flour in the summer kitchen.

40 | 41

Many pilgrims walk for several days to attend the shaman festival. The variety of faces and traditional costumes is witness to the immigration of different ethnic groups into the Nepali Langtang and Helambu areas during the last 300 years.

76 | 77

The world's largest thangka of Namdroling Monastery in South India in detail.

50 | 51

In the early morning hours, pilgrims take their purifying bath in the Gosainkund lake in honor of Shiva, Vishnu and Brahma.

78 | 79

"May peace prevail on earth." Monks in front of a store's roller shutter in Dharamsala.

58 | 59

The novices of Phunaka Dzong in Bhutan studying for their exams. They are in the mood for fun and games because the discipline master has just left the room.

90 | 91

With arms open wide, Mahakala is dancing in the courtyard of Wang-di Dzong in Bhutan.

92 | 93

Security police is omnipresent at the Jokhang in Lhasa's old part. A young girl is performing prostrations around the Jokhang, wearing a leather apron and wooden protections for the flats of her hands. The money in her left hand has been donated by Tibetans in honor of her meritorious action.

120 | 121

Tongza Dzong in central Bhutan, the very first dzong of the country, built in 1647 by Shabrung, the founder of the kingdom. Situated 2,200 meters (7,216 feet) high, the dzong is an architectural masterpiece. Bhutan's royal family has its origins in the dynasty of Tongza Dzong, which, due to its location in central Bhutan, has been the focal point of power since the beginning.

94 | 95

In the morning and evening hours, Tibetans come to pray at the Potala Palace. The old woman has put down her prayer wheel while she is prostrating herself again and again before the Potala. The Chinese propaganda in front of her says: "The development of tourism in Tibet makes economy flourish. The Tourist Bureau of Lhasa."

122 | 123

The French woman Alexandra David-Néel was the first European woman to travel the roof of the world at the beginning of the 20th century. For a long time, she also lived in Sikkim. Travel guide Mongallana Singhi proudly presents a photograph showing Alexandra David-Néel and her adopted son Jongzen. They are said to have stayed in room number two more than 80 years ago. Opposite: two old nuns in the yard of Rumtek Monastery.

106 | 107

Going from Lhasa to Shigatse by way of the Southern route, one passes the new water reservoir between Karo La and Gyantse. Here a nunnery comes into sight, which has been completely destroyed during the Cultural Revolution.

134 | 135

In Druk Sangak Choling Monastery in Darjeeling there are huge brass prayer wheels which are moved by means of ropes connected to swing bearings. To keep them constantly turning is a task especially for the elderly, who spend many days in a row concentrated on this job.

108 | 109

On the way to Mount Kailash in the West of Tibet, one encounters large herds of yaks time and time again.

136 | 137

Since ten years ago, the possession or presentation of Dalai Lama photographs has been prohibited. Nevertheless, one comes to meet pilgrims on the way who keep a picture of the Dalai Lama hidden on their body and proudly present it to the camera, like here in the Kailash area.

138 | 139

On our kora around Mount Kailash, we meet a nun of the Bon tradition who comes from the opposite direction. She has been prostrating all the way for 18 days, and it is for the 18th time that she has performed the kora by means of prostration. In the background, the snowy South face peak of the 'Snow Jewel' shines brightly.

164 | 165

A pilgrim at Lake Manasarovar. Even during the warm summer months, the ice on the surface never completely melts away due to the bitter-cold nights and strong winds. The temperatures in this barren landscape without much vegetation reach 30 degrees Celsius during the day, very often even more, but at night they fall considerably.

148 | 149

Sunset at Mount Kailash' North face. One can enjoy this view from Dirapuk Monastery on many a night.

166 | 167

Sometimes children are born even while on a journey. It is definitely a perfectly normal situation to go on pilgrimage with the whole family. It does not matter at all how young or how old one is, as with this family here at the monastery wall at Lake Manasarovar's Northern shore.

150 | 151

At an altitude of 5,895 meters (19,335 feet) in the inner mandala, we find a golden Tara statue. Wrapped in an old katak, the auspicious Tibetan scarf, it is surrounded by tsatsas, which are offerings made of clay, by paper money and butter lamps. The Tara rests on a rock ledge, which has been chiseled out of Mount Kailash' South face.

176 | 177

A Chinese soldier proudly presents the fish he caught in Lake Manasarovar. An intolerable sight for any Tibetan because the fish of Manasarovar are considered sacred. For Tibetans it is unthinkable to consume them as food.

152 | 153

A thundercloud mystically veils Mount Kailash, leaving just the peak of ice and snow visible. The Gods do not allow the eyes of all to fall upon it. Never has anybody put one's feet on its peak. May humanity continue to pay its respect and allow Mount Kailash its last secret.

178 | 179

CAPTIONS 183

Ladakh

Area	97,000 square kilometers (60,140 miles) (38,000 thereof, the Aksai Chin area, has been claimed by China since 1958)
Population	140,000
Capital	Leh
State system	Federal democratic parliamentary republic. Ladakh and Zanskar have been part of a federal state of the Indian Union since 1934
Religions	Tibetan Buddhism, Islam
Languages	Ladakhi, Zanskari, Urdu and various local dialects

Regional Geography

Ladakh and Zanskar as a district of the Indian federal state Jammu & Kashmir are under one administration, but geographically they are dif-

ferent. Situated on both sides of the Indus River between the Karakorum and Himalaya mountain ranges at an average of 3,500 meters (11,480 feet) altitude, Ladakh and Zanskar are characterized by high arid plains with little vegetation in an extremely dry climate. The 7,672-meter (25,164 feet) Saser Kangri is the highest peak. Colorful grasses and flowers grow along brooks of melt water from the high plains. During the short summer, temperatures rise up to 30 degrees Celsius, whereas in winter, in extreme cases, they can fall to minus 40 degrees. Even within one day, temperatures can greatly change. In spite of these difficult climatic conditions, wolf, bear, wild ass and the rare snow leopard, as well as the hardier horned animals like chamois, goat, antelope and blue sheep are native to Ladakh and Zanskar.

History and Politics

As part of the Tibetan Empire, Ladakh became an independent kingdom in the beginning of the 11th century, whose ruler supported the Buddhist religion and had the first monasteries constructed as religious centers according to the Tibetan example. Due to the teachings of the Indian tantric Padmasambhava, Buddhism had already taken ground in Ladakh in the 8th century. Internal differences in the Ladakhi royal court ruined the country's stability during the 15th century, to the effect that it ended up in chaos. Not before 1470, the rulers of the Namgyal dynasty once more took the reins and directed the region's destiny for 400 years. In 1834, Ladakh was defeated by the attacks of the Indian Dogra and handed over to the Raj of Jammu a few years later. During the Kashmir conflict, which has been going on since 1949, India as well as Pakistan have laid claim on the area. Therefore, Ladakh has been involved in the conflict since the Indian independence, and aggression between Buddhists and Muslims keeps flaring up. Further fuel for conflict is the occupation of the Aksai Chin region by the Chinese in 1962. Ladakh's claims for autonomy are strictly opposed within the Indian administrative bureaucracy, except for small concessions.

Population and Culture

Mirroring their past, Ladakhis are a mixture of the Indo-Aryan Dard and Tibetans. Their close relation with nature and the view that they are part of creation has given rise to deep religious sentiments, which pervade society's everyday life as well as tradition, art and culture. Except for some half-nomads, the larger part of the population lives in settlements. Cultural life in the Zanskar region, which is very sparsely populated and during wintertime cut off for months, equals pretty much that of Ladakh.

Economy and Industry

Besides trade, international tourism and the military as employers, agriculture and livestock farming play the decisive roles for securing people's livelihood. However, due to the high altitude and aridity, farming is only possible over an area of 236 square kilometers (91,12 square miles). Terraced fields with refined irrigation systems make the cultivation of cereals and vegetables possible up to an altitude of 4,500 meters (14,760 feet). During the short summer time apricot- and walnut-trees flourish in lower and protected areas.

Links

www.buddhanetz.org/projekte/ladakh.html
www.hrb.at/pakistan/ind_leh.html
www.baukunst.tuwien.ac.at/ladakh
www.hlade.com/lingshed_homepage
www.ladakh-tourism.com

Further information:
www.dieter-glogowski.de, "Himalaya Forum"

Nepal

Area	140,800 square kilometers (54,363 square miles)
Population	25,873,917 (July 2002)
Capital	Kathmandu
State system	Constitutional monarchy with multi-party system
Religions	Hinduism, Buddhism, Islam
Languages	Nepali, 12 further languages and about 30 local dialects

Regional Geography

Nepal's landscape consists of three main regions at altitudes between 70 and 8,850 meters (230 and 29,028 feet – Mount Everest): the lowlands occupy 20 percent, the medium-altitude grounds 15 percent, the high-mountain region 65 percent of Nepal's total area. Monsoon and high altitude dominate the climatic conditions of these different areas. Tropical heat, moderate zones and arctic cold produce a variety of animals and plants which are well adapted to their respective regions. Whether crocodile or snow leopard, whether bamboo jungle or edelweiss, they are all at home in Nepal.

History and Politics

In 1768, the territory of Nepal, which consisted of three separate kingdoms, was unified by a Gurkha ruler. Following clashes with the British, a British mission was installed in Kathmandu in 1816. Although outwardly strong, domestic fighting destabilized the country. An upstart took the chance and appointed himself prime minister with far reaching authority. The king himself was thus degraded as a puppet. These power structures did not change until 1951 whereupon King Tribhuvan reinstalled monarchy. The first parliamentary elections, however, were undermined by King Tribhuvan's successor King Mahendra. He substituted democratic structures with a system void of political par-

ties, which secured his full authority. In 1972, King Birendra, a liberally minded politician, took over government. Supported by a new constitution, he established a constitutional monarchy in 1991. The effects of the Maoist guerilla movement, which has been active for several years, the claims of the "Movement for the Reinstallation of Democracy," and the assassination of King Birendra in 2001, currently deprive Nepal of its domestic stability.

Population and Culture

Nepal is a melting pot of markedly different ethnic groups of Indian-Aryan and Tibetan-Burmese origin. The Newari, popular for their woodcarving skills, have had a particular influence on the culture of the Kathmandu Valley. Like the majority of the population, they are followers of Hinduism as well, whereas the Sherpa, who have originally emigrated from Tibet, have preserved the genuine influence of Tibetan Buddhism in their culture. In remote places of Nepal, like the area where the Tamang settle, the Bon religion is still alive.

Economy and Industry

In terms of gross national product, Nepal is one of the poorest nations on earth. Since 2001, the bad economical situation has become worse

due to domestic tensions; and the prospects are dark. The most important economic sector is agriculture, although only 20 percent of the country can be cultivated. Some industry has developed from the processing of agricultural crops like jute, sugar cane, tobacco and cereals, but with a few exceptions, it is currently losing its importance. Nepal's efforts to attract foreign investment is mostly undermined by mistrust due to the political and economic instability. This has an effect also on the sector of tourism, which has been the most important foreign exchange earner in recent years. Connected to the aftermath of the 2001 terror attacks on the US, statistics and balances show alarmingly bad figures.

Tip: For 15 years now, Shiva Shresta has accompanied Dieter Glogowski as a reliable guide and meanwhile as a good friend on his tours through the Himalaya region. Shiva organizes and guides groups of two to four persons from his home base in Kathmandu.

Links

www.nepal.de
www.dieter-glogowski.de, "Himalaya Forum"
www.baukunst.tuwien.ac.at/ladakh
www.hlade.com/lingshed_homepage
www.ladakh-tourism.com

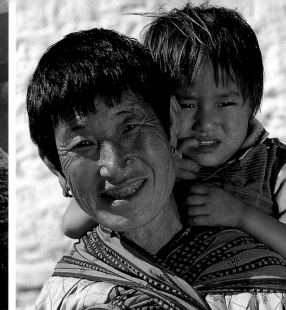

Bhutan

Area	47,000 square kilometers (18,147 square miles)
Population	2,094,176 (July 2002)
Capital	Thimphu
State system	Constitutional monarchy
Religions	Tibetan Buddhism, Hinduism
Languages	Dzongkha (official language), Tibetan, and Nepali dialects

Regional Geography
The kingdom is situated in the Eastern Himalaya region. It shares the Northern border with Tibet and the Southern, Eastern and Western borders with India. The inhabitants themselves call their nation Druk Yul, Land of the Dragon. In spite of the relatively small size of the country, the profile of its landscape is characterized by three different climatic zones. According to the subtropical, moderate and alpine grounds, flora and fauna are varied. There are altitudes between 200 and 7,554 meters (656 and 24,777 feet) Kulha Gangri). Precipitation varies between 500 and 5,000 milliliters per year, depending on monsoon and part of the country. Bhutan has the same latitude as central Egypt.

History and Politics
The tantric master Padmasambhava, who had earlier on introduced Buddhism in Tibet, also went on to establish this in Bhutan in the 8th century. At the beginning of the 9th century, a wave of immigrants from the Buddhist North stabilized the religion further. Among the various Buddhist traditions that were developing, the Drukpa Kagyu school maintained its position. Thus it also was a Drukpa monk who in the 17th century laid the foundation of a unified nation with a dual government system. Tibetan Buddhism became the state religion. Domestic tensions that kept flaring up, coupled with the increasing interference of the British during the 18th and 19th century, lead to the replacement of the old government system by a hereditary monarchy.

In 1949, Bhutans's independency was formally acknowledged by India. The third king of Bhutan, Jigme Dorji Wangchuk, established and gradually implemented a policy of openness and reform. Combined with the preservation of culture and tradition, and with environmentally compatible modernization, this policy has been continued by his son, His Majesty Jigme Singhye Wangchuk, since 1972. The campaign for Bhutanization, which was initiated in 1989 to drive ethnic minorities out of the country, remains a controversial issue.

Population and Culture
Bhutan's population does not form an ethnical unit, but consists of about 50 percent Bhutia, 35 percent Nepali and 15 percent other origins. Thus besides the official language Dzongkha, for which a written form has existed for 30 years only, there is a Babel of languages and dialects. The rate of illiteracy is 57.8 percent. Close juxtaposition of religion, politics and everyday life is characteristic for Bhutan. The highest spiritual dignitary, the Je Khenpo, has a say in religious as well as in worldly matters. Monasteries and monastic fortresses (Dzongs) are important institutions for the population. Not only as centers of religious life but also as hubs of administration and general market-like meeting points, they play an important role in social life. Due to the isolation and merely reluctant opening of the country, the traditional way of life has been preserved nearly unaltered over the centuries. The focal point of life is the family, in which women enjoy high status.

Economy and Industry
Due to a rural population of about 85 percent, agriculture, which cultivates 8 percent of the overall area, is the dominating sector of economy. The importance of craftsmanship, industry and the service sector is relatively small. Among exports like cement, timber, fruits and spices, electricity is the most important because Bhutan has large resources of waterpower. Besides the extension of infrastructure, the development of industry and trade is a major objective.

Links
www.kingdomofbhutan.com
www.dse.de/za/lis/bhutan
www.helvetas.org.bt
www.amnesty.org/report2004/
    Btn-summary-eng
www.dieter-glogowski.de, "Himalaya Forum"

Sikkim

Area	7,096 square kilometers (2,740 square miles)
Population	540,500 (2001)
Capital	Gangtok
State system	Federal democratic parliamentary republic. Sikkim is a federal state of the Indian Union
Languages	Lepcha, Bhutia, Nepali, Hindi and Limboo
Religions	Hinduism, Tibetan Buddhism

Regional Geography

Sikkim's landscape is characterized by extreme differences in altitude and by different climatic zones. The country shares its borders with Tibet, Bhutan, Nepal and West Bengal. The terrain climbs from 228 meters (748 feet) in the subtropical river valley of the Tista up to more than 8,000 meters (26,240 feet) into alpine climate. The Kangchendzonga, Sikkim's highest peak, is the third highest mountain of the world; it is revered as a protective deity. The monsoon-dependent region has precipitations of up to 6,000 millimeters (19 feet) per year. The landscape, which ranges from lush green vegetation to permanent ice, is as varied as the species-richness of animals and plants. Among the more than 4,000 varieties of plants, there are 600 different kinds of orchids alone. Sikkim's nature offers rare species a space to live, like the red Panda, the endemic Schapis and many others.

History and Politics

Since the 13th century, Tibetans have immigrated to Sikkim, the home of the Lepcha. In 1642, the state system of a monarchy came into being. During the following 300 years, many conflicts with Bhutan, Nepal and the British colonial power lead to the repeated loss of territory. Eventually, the British intervened in order to check domestic aggression within Sikkim's population and to limit the wave of immigrants from Nepal, which threatened to overrun the kingdom. In 1890, Sikkim was declared a British protectorate, which was taken over by India in 1950. With the fall of King Chogyal, who became the focus of general suspicion due to his marriage with an American, the status of a kingdom was lost. By means of an alteration of the constitution, the kingdom was integrated into the Indian Union as a federal state in 1975. The Chinese have not accepted India's new border and interpreted the change of status as an annexation. Until today the Sikkim issue has not been resolved between the two powers.

Population and Culture

Since the 19th century, the ethnic groups of the Lepcha and the Bhotia, who have lived in Sikkim for centuries, have been confronted with massive immigration waves from Nepal, to the effect that they are minorities today. Currently, about 80 percent of Sikkim's population are Nepali. Besides their traditions, culture and Hinduist religion, the immigrants have introduced effective agricultural methods like the terracing of fields. Everyday life and religion are closely connected with each other in Sikkim, with elements of Hinduism and Buddhism mixing. According to statistics, 40 percent of the population exists below the poverty limit. The rate of illiteracy is about 30 percent.

Economy and Industry

Agriculture cultivating 15 percent of the overall area is the main pillar of economy and feeds about two thirds of the population. Statistics vary as to the spread of the rural population, ranging between 70 and 90 percent. Besides the sectors of forestry, fishery and livestock farming, there is cultivation of cereals, tea, cotton and spices, among which cardamom and ginger are the most important exports. Compared to the production of electricity from water-power, the mining of natural resources like coal, quartz, graphite, copper and other minerals is substantially less. The marketing of industrially produced merchandise has reluctantly developed. Here, Sikkim is hoping for foreign investments. The government considers

tourism as a sector with potential growth. Sikkim's culture and especially its nature offers abundant opportunities for international tourism in terms of leisure and sports.

Links

www.sikkiminfo.net
www.sikkimchildren.org

Further information:

www.dieter-glogowski.de, "Himalaya Forum"

Tibet

Area	1,228,440 square kilometers (4,668,07 square miles)
Population	2,520,000
Capital	Lhasa
State system	Autonomous republic of the People's Republic of China
Religions	Tibetan Buddhism
Languages	Tibetan, Chinese (official language)

Regional Geography

With the proclamation of the Autonomous Republic of Tibet in 1965, large areas of the historical territory, which formerly belonged to Tibet, were incorporated into Chinese provinces. Today, Tibet's area comprises less than half of its original territory. Situated between the Kunlun mountain range in the North, the Himalaya in the West, and adjoining India, Nepal, Myanmar and Bhutan in the South, it is the largest high plain in the world with an average altitude of 4,500 meters (14,760 feet). The Transhimalaya mountain range is a meteorological divide separating the dry steppes of the North with their tempera- ture fluctuations between minus 40 degrees Celsius in wintertime and 35 degrees in sum- mertime, from the climatically favored valleys in the South. Tibet's vegetation is rather sparse, as opposed to the rich population of animals and their varying species.

History and Politics

Tibet's historical era began in the 7th century with the unification of Tibetan tribes by Songt- sen Gampo, who declared Buddhism the state religion. Since the middle of the 9th century, the country was destabilized by religious war- fare between the followers of the animistic Bon religion and Bud- dhism; thereby it split up into several small principalities. It was not before the 10th century that Buddhist monasteries gained influence once more. Tsongkha- pa, the great reformer of disci- pline for Buddhist monks and founder of the Gelugpa school, established the basis for the later theocratic state system, whose head has carried the title Dalai Lama since the middle of the 16th century. China's support against the invasion of the Dsun- gar from East Turkestan in 1717 has had consequences until today. In the time following, the Chinese considered Tibet to be their protectorate. Only around 1911, during the Chinese revolution, Tibet succeeded in expelling the powerful neighbor temporarily. China's government has never acknowledged Tibet's independence on the grounds of history. In 1950, the Chinese People's Liberation Army invaded Tibet and proceeded to occupy the cap- ital Lhasa in 1951, after the signing of the "Sev- enteen-Point Agreement." In the process, Tibet was formally assured of domestic autonomy. Eight years later, the 14th Dalai Lama escaped into exile in India, followed by 80,000 Tibetans.

Population and Culture

Everyday life of the Tibetans is characterized by deep religiosity. Since China's occupation, how- ever, Tibetan traditions are subject to severe restrictions. By means of an active settlement policy, the Chinese population is increasing and playing a leading role in decision-making; China's policy of "liberation and modernization" does not only mean construction of roads, schools or hospitals, but at the same time destruction of the Tibetan culture, suppression and gradual extermination of the Tibetan peo- ple as well as exploitation of the environment. That in Kham and Amdo, regions in the East of the historical Tibet, 60 percent of the forests have been cleared during the last 30 years; and that the country is used as a refuse dump for nuclear waste and other chemical residue, to name only two examples, is bound to lead to severe consequences.

Economy and Industry

Tibet's natural resources like zinc, lead, copper, iron and other raw materials have, to a large extent, not been mined so far. Agriculture is the most important source of employment. Besides hemp, Soya beans and cotton, the limited farm- land is cultivated with potatoes and various kinds of vegetables, fruits and cereals. Yaks, sheep and goats are animals which are well adapt to the high altitude and therefore suit- able for livestock farming. Even today, the industry is confined to small production units for textiles, wood and metal products.

Links
www.tibet-initiative.de
www.tibetfreunde.ch, www.tibetfocus.com
www.dieter-glogowski.de, "Himalaya Forum"

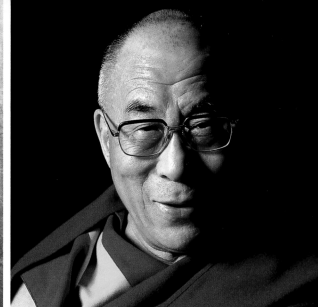

Tibet in Exile

On his escape from Tibet, the 14th Dalai Lama reached the Indian border on April 18, 1959. He left his country like through a cloud of mist, he says, sick, exhausted and much more desperate than he ever would be able to express. Since the invasion of the Chinese in 1950, the tense political situation had considerably deteriorated within a few years. When the signs of an attempted abduction of His Holiness became obvious, the only solution was the way into exile. Under the condition that he would refrain from any political activity, the Indian government granted His Holiness refuge. Within a short time, about 80,000 Tibetans followed their leader to India.

Establishment of an Exile Government

In 1960, the Dalai Lama found a new home in the village of McLeod Ganji above Dharamsala in the Indian federal state of Himachal Pradesh. There, he has gradually established an exile government based on a new constitution which relied on Buddhist principles and the International Declaration of Human Rights. Over the course of time, the institutions related to a democratic system were installed. Besides a parliament with directly elected representatives, there is a cabinet with ministers appointed by the Dalai Lama, who are responsible for the following departments: religious and cultural matters, education, finance and economy, health, information, and security.

Tibetans in Exile

Until today, the wave of refugees from Tibet has not fully subsided. As to the statistics, well over 120,000 people have succeeded to escape; but these are just a fraction of those who have made the attempt. In spite of international support, the conditions in the transit camps in Nepal, Sikkim, Bhutan and India in the sixties and seventies were horrible. For many, humanitarian aid came too late. Moreover, the smaller countries of the Himalaya region, due to domestic problems, were not capable of granting refuge to the Tibetans; so they had to be distributed and resettled. For many this was another traumatic situation because adapting to the tropical heat of South India's jungles was for the people from the roof of the world once more a matter of survival.

Today, about 90,000 Tibetans live in North and South India, 10,000 in Nepal, 1,000 in Bhutan, 3,000 in Europe, mostly in Switzerland, and a few in the US. Their living conditions and problems are considerably different depending on where they stay. Some Tibetans in Switzerland manage small businesses enjoying the according living standard. In other countries, they live in poor conditions. Due to the enjoyable cultural surrounding, Tibetans in North India are more successful in preserving their identity and their cultural heritage than those in Switzerland or in the US, where integration into the society and making a living on the one hand and cultivating their own traditions on the other hand cannot always be successfully combined. It is a great loss, for example, when Tibetan children cannot speak Tibetan anymore.

The Exile Government's activities

Besides social care for newly arriving refugees, education of children and young people, and the thoughtful care and housing of the many orphans, one of the most difficult tasks of the exile government is to mobilize the international public for the struggle toward the enforcement of international law. Until today, the discussions of the Tibet issue on international committees has not lead to any improvements worth mentioning. The struggle for Tibet's real autonomy, for tolerance among nations and religions has so far lead to nothing but appeals without obligation. The latest developments concerning actual international support are more worrying than hopeful. In the spring time of 2003, the Nepali government for

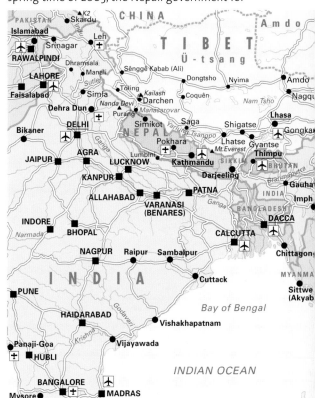

the first time followed Beijing's demand and extradited 18 Tibetan refugees to China.

Links

www.tibet.com (official website of Tibet's exile government in Dharamsala)
www.dharamsalanet.com

Further information:

www.dieter-glogowski.de, "Himalaya Forum"

Glossary

Amitabha One of the five meditation deities of the →Mahayana, originating from the elemental Buddha. Amitabha is the source of light and life.

Arhat skt. "who is worthy of veneration." A saint who has during his life time reached →Nirvana, the attainment of the →Hinayana, and will not be reborn in cyclic existences. In the →Mahayana there is the idea of the →Bodhisattva, who remains in the world until the arrival of the next →Buddha.

Avalokiteshvara →Buddha of compassion, a meditation deity and Tibet's protecting deity. →Bodhisattva.

Bardo The condition between death and rebirth. According to Tibetan psychology, after the death of the body the mind remains in an intermediate state for 49 days. At the end of this period, it is decided into which of the six realms of cyclic existence, →Samsara, one is reborn.

Bardo Thodol The Tibetan Book of the Dead. It is said to have been hidden by →Padmasambhava as a →Terma. It has been used in Tibet since the 14th century.

Barkhor Circuit for circumambulating the →Jokhang.

Bodhicitta skt. "mind of enlightenment." In the →Mahayana the altruistic striving for enlightenment for the benefit of all sentient beings.

Bodhisattva skt. "enlightened being." A practitioner of the → Mahayana or the →Vajrayana on the way to Buddhahood, motivated by →Bodhicitta. An enlightened being helping others on the path to Buddhahood.

Bonpo Pre-Buddhist belief in the Himalaya region. A nature religion characterized by animistic and magical elements.

Brahma Supreme deity in the Hindu trinity of Brahma, Vishnu and →Shiva.

Brahmin Priest or scholar in the Hinduistic caste system.

Buddha skt. "the awakened one." Epithet of enlightened beings like the historical Buddha Shakyamuni, his predecessor, and the Buddha Maitreya who is expected to appear at the end of the present era.

Chang Beer from barley.

Chorten tib.; skt. "stupa" – "basis of veneration." Buddhist reliquary.

Dalai Lama "Ocean of Wisdom." Mongolian epithet, which was granted to the third leader of the →Gelugpa by Altan Khan. Religious and political head of Tibet since the 5th Dalai Lama (1617 – 1682). The Dalai Lama is considered as an incarnation of →Avalokiteshvara and as a reincarnation of his respective predecessor.

Dhammapada skt. "path of the →Dharma." Old Buddhist scripture of the Pali canon. It contains the vital points of the →Buddha's teachings.

Dharma skt. "duty, law." Cosmic order. The body of the →Buddha's teachings. A complex notion, two aspects are the Dharma of the scriptures and the Dharma of realization, the result of spiritual practice.

Dokhang Assembly hall. Main prayer hall in Tibetan monasteries.

Dorje tib.; skt. "Vajra" →"Diamond scepter, thunder bolt." Ritual implement, a symbol of the method, the selfless engagement for the benefit of all sentient beings.

Dzong tib. "fortress." Fortified administrative center of Tibetan district governors. In Bhutan connected to large monasteries: monastic fortresses.

Eightfold Noble Path The path taught by the →Buddha to transcend the cycle of existences with its sufferings, →Samsara, by means of eight interconnected steps: right outlook, right intention, right speech, right action, right livelihood, right pursuit, right mindfulness, right concentration. These are symbolized by the eight spokes of the Wheel of →Dharma, which was set into motion by the Buddha.

Four Noble Truths Main teaching of the →Buddha during his first turning of the wheel of →Dharma. The truth of suffering, of the origin of suffering, of the cessation of suffering, and of the path to the cessation of suffering. →Eightfold Noble Path

Ganda skt. "ritual bell." Symbol of directly realized wisdom. Ganda and vajra, →Dorje, are visualized in unity during the performance of rituals.

Ganesha skt. "Lord of the Retinue of Shiva." Elephant-headed Hindu deity of wisdom, son of the goddess Parvati.

Gelugpa tib. "the virtuous ones." One of the four main schools of Tibetan Buddhism, initiated by the reformer →Tsongkhapa. The study of the scriptures and the observation of the morality connected with the monks' vows are the focus of this tradition, which is also called Yellow-Hat school.

Gompa tib. "hermitage." Temple or monastery.

Hinayana skt. "small vehicle." →Arhat. In this Buddhist tradition, the practitioner's objective of individual liberation is achieved mainly through non-violence and non-harming.

Jainism Indian religion spread by Mahavira about 500 BC, which holds that the world is not ruled by a god but by the laws of the cosmos and of morality.

Jokhang tib. "house of →Jowo." Main temple of Lhasa.

Jowo Rinpoch Highly revered statue of →Buddha Shakyamuni in the →Jokhang.

Kagyupa tib. "oral transmission." One of the four main schools of Tibetan Buddhism. The lineage was initiated by →Marpa, the teacher of →Milarepa.

Kang Rinpoche tib. "snow jewel," skt. "Kailash." The most sacred mountain of Buddhists, Hindus, Jains and →Bonpos. According to Tibetan cosmology, it corresponds to the mystical center of the universe →Meru.

Kangjur tib. "translated words." Compilation of the vast canonical scriptures of Tibetan Buddhism translated from Sanskrit.

Karma skt. "action." The law of cause and effect, which produces the conditions for rebirth.

Karmapa Head lama of Tsurphu Monastery in Central Tibet. The supreme incarnation of the Karma Kagyu school. →Kagyupa

Kora Circuit for the circumambulation of sacred places.

Lama tib. "unsurpassed." Spiritual teacher in the tradition of Tibetan Buddhism.

Lamrim tib. "gradual path." Complete description of the path to enlightenment of the →Gelugpa school.

Lingam Stones in the form of a phallus which are venerated as symbols for the creative force of the deity →Shiva.

Lingkhor The outer circuit of circumambulation in Lhasa.

Mahayana skt. "great vehicle." Buddhist path which is focused on achieving enlightenment for the benefit of all sentient beings. A practitioner of this path is called →Bodhisattva.

Mala Rosary with 108 beads. 108 is a sacred figure for Tibetans.

Mandala skt. "circle." A diagram of circular shape which symbolizes the universe and is used for the purpose of meditation.

Mani stone skt. "jewel." Carved with mantras, mani stones are often found piled up as walls near monasteries or on pilgrimage routes.

Manjushri Meditation deity and →Bodhisattva of supreme wisdom.

Mantra Formulas for meditation which are repeated over and over again, and thus protect the mind from negative thinking.

Mara skt. "murderer." The master of desire, the personification of evil.

Meru Mythical center of the universe in Indian-Tibetan cosmology. Its worldly representation is Mount Kailash. →Kang Rinpoche

Mudra skt. "symbol, seal." Symbolical hand gesture in Hinduism and Buddhism.

Nirvana skt. "state of peace." Liberation from the cyclic existences of suffering →Samsara.

Nyingmapa tib. "the old ones." One of the four main schools of Tibetan Buddhism. It goes back to Padmasambhava and the first translations of the →Buddha's teachings from Sanskrit. Also called Red-Hat school.

Panchen Lama The second highest spiritual authority of the →Gelugpa tradition after the →Dalai Lama.

Potala The palace of the Dalai Lama in Lhasa.

Puja skt. "veneration." Ceremony, ritual, service.

Rinpoche tib. "precious one." Form of address for an incarnate →Lama.

Sadhu skt. "good one." Hindu saint or monk who leads a life of asceticism.

Sakyapa One of the four main schools of Tibetan Buddhism, named after their main seat in Tibet.

Samsara skt. "migration." The wandering of sentient beings through cyclic existences which are experienced as fateful because of ignorance. →Karma

Sangha skt. "gathering." The followers of the →Buddha.

Shiva skt. "Nataraja," →"Lord of Dance." Hindu deity performing the dance of creation and destruction.

Sutra skt. "manual." Religious texts in Hinduism and the words of the →Buddha in Buddhism.

Tantra skt. "fabric." Hindu or Buddhist texts or religious systems. In Buddhism the basic scriptures of →Vajrayana.

Tara tib. "Drolma," →"saviouress." Female meditation deity, emanation of →Avalokiteshvara.

Terma tib. "hidden treasure." Scriptures or objects hidden by →Padmasambhava to be discovered centuries later when they would be most beneficial.

Vajrayana skt. "diamond vehicle." Tantric version of →Mahayana Buddhism, mainly practiced in the Tibetan cultural area.

Wheel of Life In the process of his enlightenment, →Buddha Shakyamuni realized the workings of cyclic existence, →Samsara, their causes, as well as the path to liberation. His visionary realizations are depicted in the Wheel of Life.

Yama skt. "Lord of Death." Mythical figure who will weigh the →Karma of beings.

Brief Biographies

Anagarika Govinda 1898–1985. Important German interpreter of Buddhism.

Buddha Shakyamuni 450–370 BC. Siddharta Gautama, the historical Buddha.

Dilgo Khyentse Rinpoche 1919–1991. Buddhist master of the Nyingma tradition.

Drukpa Rinpoche Tibetan meditation master of the 20th century, close friends with the Dalai Lama.

Herbert Tichy 1912–1987. Austrian geologist, journalist and author.

Jack Kornfield Born 1945. Became a meditation teacher in Asia in the 1970ies.

Kalu Rinpoche 1906–1989. Tibetan master of the Kagyu tradition.

Mahatma Gandhi 1869-1948. Indian lawyer, politician and human rights activist.

Marpa 1012–1098. Initiator of the Kagyu school.

Matthieu Ricard Born 1946. Monk and French translator of the Dalai Lama.

Milarepa 1040–1123. Tibetan tantric yogi, saint and poet. Disciple of Marpa.

Padmasambhava skt. 'the lotus-born.' Introduced Buddhism to Tibet in the 8th century. Also called Guru Rinpoche.

Pema Chödrön Born 1936 in the US. Became a Buddhist nun in 1974.

Shantideva 8th century. A Bodhisattva representing the Middle-Way philosophy.

Sogyal Rinpoche Important lama of the Nyingma tradition, who has taught in the West since 1974.

Tenzin Gyatso born 1935 in Kham. His Holiness the 14th Dalai Lama, who was awarded the Nobel Peace Prize in 1989.

Thich Nhat Hanh Born 1926. Vietnamese meditation master now living in France.

Tsongkhapa 1357–1419. Losang Dragpa. Great reformer and initiator of the Gelug school.

Acknowledgements

I would like to thank Lama Yeshe Osel for the Tibetan calligraphy and Hannelore Wenderoth for editorial support. Thank you to Irmtraut Wäger and Manfred Ochudlo of the German support group Deutsche Tibethilfe, and to my sponsors Ms Alig of Austrian Airlines, Manfred Hell and Zelinda Pahl of Jack Wolfskin, Steffen Keil and Hanns-Peter Cohn of Leica, and Maike Reinhardt of Kodak. I am especially grateful to His Holiness the 14th Dalai Lama and his secretary Tenzin Geyche, and to Sogyal Rinpoche and Sonam Yospel for their contributions to this book.

Source Materials of Quotations
Ama Adhe: The Voice that Remembers, 1999
Bauer: Irgendwo in Bhutan. Waldgut 1994
Binder, Rode: Tibet. Hirmer 2000
Binder: Kailash – Reise zum Berg der Götter. dtv 2002
Brauen: Traumwelt Tibet. Haupt 2000
Mary Craig: Tears of Blood – A Cry for Tibet. 2001
Dilgo Khyentse: Enlightened Courage. Editions Padmakara 1992
Dilgo Khyentse: The Heart Treasure of the Enlightened Ones. Shambala Publications 1992
Walter Y. Evans-Wentz: Tibet's Great Yogi Milarepa. 2000
Faber: Tibetisches Tagebuch. Heyne 1996
Föllmi: Die Weisheiten des Buddhismus Tag für Tag. Knesebeck 2003
Fritz, Gerasimou: Sikkim. DeGe-Verlag 1997
Govinda: The Way of the White Clouds. London 1966
Johnson, Moran: Kailash – Der heilige Berg Tibets, Bruckmann 2001
Kalu Rinpoche: Gently Whispered. Station Hill Press 1994
Matthieu Ricard: Journey to Enlightenment – The Life and World of Khyentse Rinpoche, Spiritual Teacher from Tibet. 1996
Mythos Tibet. Dumont 1997
Kazuyochi Nomachi: Tibet. 1997
Shantideva: The Way of the Bodhisattva. Shambala Publications 1997
Sogyal Rinpoche: Glimpse after Glimpse – Daily Reflections on Living and Dying. San Francisco 1995
Sogyal Rinpoche: The Tibetan Book of Living and Dying. San Francisco 1992
Weihreter: Westhimalaya. Adeva-Verlag 2001
Wilhelmy: Bhutan. Beck'sche Reihe 1990 Durchgesehene Nachauflage 2006

Imprint

Co-writers

Franz Binder is a freelance writer and photojournalist based in Munich. Among the 23 books he has published until today in the field of belletristic and informative literature, there are two novels as well as illustrated books on Central Asia and the Tibetan cultural area.

Klemens Ludwig, born in 1955 in the German Sauerland region, is a freelance journalist. He has traveled Tibet and published several books, newspaper articles as well as radio programs on the subject. Moreover, he is in close contact with the Tibetans in exile, namely in North India and Switzerland. From 1994 to 2000, he was the head of the German support group Tibet Initiative Deutschland.

Katharina Sommer, born in 1958, is an editor, a review writer and a freelance journalist. Specialized in the fields of Asia and Eastern Europe, she works for daily newspapers, specialist publications, tourism boards, as well as for individual writers. In her publications, she is particularly committed to her cause concerning the inhabitants of the Himalaya region.

 my point of view

Further information on Dieter Glogowski's projects, talks and exhibitions: www.dieter-glogowski.de

We are always grateful for suggestions and advice. Please send your comments to:
C.J. Bucher Publishing, Product Management
Innsbrucker Ring 15, 81673 Munich, Germany
E-mail: editorial@bucher-publishing.com
Homepage: www.bucher-publishing.com

Photography and text: Dieter Glogowski, Friedberg, Germany
Translation and editing: Hannelore Wenderoth, Bad Camberg, Germany
Proof-reading: Brian Leonard, Bad Goisern, Austria
Design: Albrecht Haag, Darmstadt, Germany
Calligraphy: Lama Yeshe Osel
Cartography: Gecko Maps, Hinteregg, Switzerland
Product management for the English edition: Dr. Birgit Kneip
Production: Bettina Schippel
Repro: Scanner Service, Verona, Italy
Printed in Slovenia by MKT Print, Ljubljana

ISBN 978-3-7658-1634-5

See our full listing of books at
www.bucher-publishing.com